KINDLING
for the
FIRE

Meditations to Warm the Heart
and Ignite the Spirit

bright sky press
HOUSTON, TEXAS

2365 Rice Blvd., Suite 202
Houston, Texas 77005

Library of Congress Cataloging-in-Publication Data on file with publisher.

ISBN 978-1-936474-08-0

10   9   8   7   6   5   4   3   2   1

Editorial Direction, Lucy Herring Chambers
Creative Direction, Ellen Peeples Cregan
Design, Marla Garcia

Printed in Canada through Friesens

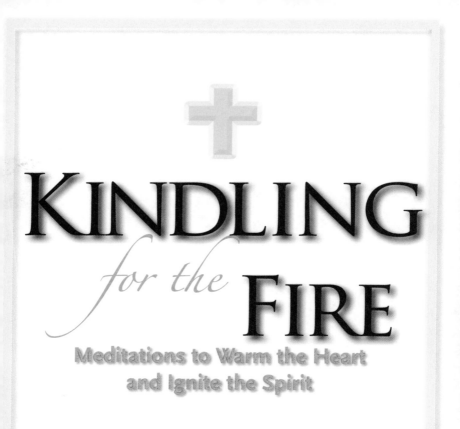

KINDLING
for the FIRE

Meditations to Warm the Heart and Ignite the Spirit

DWIGHT EDWARDS

bright sky press
HOUSTON, TEXAS

To my beloved wife, Lauri

Table of Contents

Introduction 8

Chapter 1
Radiance—Fire's Beauty 11

Chapter 2
Fragance—Fire's Aroma 33

Chapter 3
The Fire Triangle—Fire's Triumvirate 55

Chapter 4
Firewood—Fire's Community 75

Chapter 5
Fuel—Fire's Resourcing 95

Chapter 6
Flames—Fire's Essence 117

Chapter 7
The Hearth—Fire's Homestead 139

Chapter 8
Sparks—Fire's Emissaries 163

Chapter 9
Light—Fire's Brilliance 185
Chapter 10
Heat—Fire's Warmth 207
Chapter 11
Shadows—Fire's Flickering 227
Chapter 12
Longevity—Fire's Tenacity 249
Conclusion 269
Bibliography 273

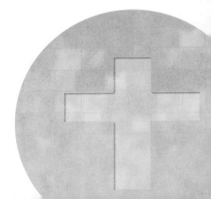

Introduction

"**What fire is this that warms my soul?...O fire that burns forever, and never dies, kindle me! O light which shines eternally, and never darkens, illumine me... How sweetly do you burn!**" Augustine

Fire. There are many pictures used for God in the Bible—rock, water, wind, fortress, refuge, etc. But the similitude which outstrips all of them is one that we probably wouldn't expect. It is that of *fire*. Over ninety times God and His presence are likened unto fire. *"For our God is a consuming fire,"* writes the author of Hebrews, and both the Old and New Testaments camp heavily upon this blazing portrait. However, God is not only a fire on the outside; He is equally a fire on the inside. And were that not true, I would not have written this book. Let me explain.

This book is founded upon one central, bedrock conviction: There is a permanent, inextinguishable fire in every believer's soul. A God-birthed fire...a Spirit-sustained fire...a Christ-adoring fire. It is a holy fire; a gifted fire for which we can take no credit. Its flames can never be fully doused, regardless of the amount of sin, rebellion, confusion, or idolatry in our lives. This fire yearns to enflame every facet of our being but will not go where it is not invited. It is a gentle fire. It is a kind fire. But make no mistake; it is also a jealous fire. A fire that violently protests every vestige of sin in our lives while delighting deeply in our every small, faltering movement towards the Lover of our souls.

This fire is the living, breathing, actual presence of God in the deep recesses of our being. In reality it is a *Him,* not an *it.* As Dante put it, we are *"ingodded."* The God whose presence set ablaze a desert bush when He spoke to Moses is the same God Who has taken up fiery residency within us. Therefore, our calling as fire-indwelt saints is not to work to keep the fire lit. The fire is here to stay; it is as incapable of going out as God is of dying. We are permanently *"sealed by the Holy Spirit for the day of redemption,"* as the apostle Paul writes. But every fire needs kindling. Every flame needs a boost now and again. And that, my friend, is exactly what this book is all about.

Kindling for the Fire. The title pretty well conveys what my hopes are for this book. It is simply firewood for the fire within. If you have entered into a personal relationship with Jesus Christ through trusting in Him alone for the forgiveness of your sins, then you are on fire. You are not only assured of eternity in heaven, you are equally assured of permanent indwelling on earth. Permanent indwelling by the very Author of the universe, the very Son of God, *"very God of very God,"* as the Nicene Creed puts it. On your very worst days you are no less indwelt and on your very best days you are not one iota more indwelt. There is a heavenly fire within you, my friend, which is not going anywhere. And until we hit heaven, this fire will not rest content until we are wholly swallowed up in His joyous, holy, strong conflagration.

The devotions contained in these pages are simply de-signed to add some fuel to the fire that is already burn-ing within you. They are not logs; they really are kindling. What I mean by this is that they are intentionally short. My underlying philosophy in writing can be summed up in nine words—*Get in quick. Leave something substantial. Get out quick.* I hope that I've accomplished this in at least some measure. The book is divided into twelve sections, each focusing on a different aspect of fire. This was my publish-er's idea and I think it is a great one. Let me encourage you to read these meditations slowly, focusing primarily on the scriptures given within each. Many of these devotions are written to encourage. Some to provoke deeper self-examination. Others are penned to challenge widely held paradigms that need to be re-examined. And still others are devoted to simply equipping. But all of them are writ-ten with the highest hopes that the Spirit of Christ will use these words to draw you into His arms more deeply, to cause you to feast on His presence more passionately, and to compel you to depend upon His resources more desperately. With the hopes that they will indeed serve as spiritual kindling for the Great Fire within. And that this heavenly blaze will find its way through you to the many who need your same gifted fire.

God bless you my friend, as you slowly journey through these pages.

Radiance

FIRE'S BEAUTY

"Life has loveliness to sell,
All beautiful and splendid things,
Blue waves whitened on a cliff,
Soaring fire that sways and sings,
And children's faces looking up
Holding wonder like a cup."

– SARA TEASDALE –

As a child I could sit by our fireplace and watch its logs burn for hours on end. There is an exquisite beauty to fire; a non-stop radiance that captivates the sight as well as warms the body. Under its mesmerizing spell I could forget about the troubles and pressures of my eight-year-old world and take concerted delight in the bright, dancing colors which seemed to perform solely for me.

Fire in the spiritual life represents many things—light, warmth, power, etc. But certainly, certainly it must also represent beauty. Radiant beauty. First and foremost, it is the unrivaled splendor of the triune God of whom it is said, "He is altogether lovely" (Song of Songs 5:16). It is also the Spirit-bestowed beauty that characterizes the lives and dealings of all of God's children. This is what St. Francis Assisi was alluding to in his famous line, "Preach the gospel at all times. If necessary use words." In more modern times, Christian philosopher Francis Schaeffer put it like this, "The local church or Christian group should be right, but it should also be beautiful. The local group should be the example of the supernatural, of the substantially healed relationship in this present life between men and men."

The following meditations center on radiance—fire's beauty.

Beauty

"The works of the LORD are great, studied by all who have pleasure in them. His work is honorable and glorious..."
Ps. 111:2-3

Nobody, but *nobody* should be greater lovers of nature than believers. Of all peoples, we should lead the pack in adoring, relishing, and insatiably enjoying the handiwork of God with every fiber of our created being. Note the psalmist's words—*"studied by all who have pleasure in them."* Not "who have *interest* in them," nor "who have *curiosity* in them". The Hebrew word for *"pleasure"* means exactly that—emotional delight. I love the way Eugene Peterson translates this verse in *The Message: "God's works are so great, worth a lifetime of study—endless enjoyment! Splendor and beauty mark his craft..."* The poet Elizabeth Barrett Browning puts it beautifully:

Earth is crammed with heaven,
and every common bush is on fire with God;
but only he who sees takes off his shoes;
the rest sit around it and pluck blackberries.

The heavens and their stars trumpet forth His grandeur; the earth and all that is within it proudly show off His craftsmanship. Where else are we going to go to find the kind of eye-stopping beauty enthralling enough to satisfy our eternal spirits? The theologian and prolific writer

Frederick Buechner notes concerning our need for beauty, *"It is to the spirit what food is to the flesh. It fills an emptiness in you that nothing else under the sun can."*

We are born into this world beauty starved. There is within every man and woman an undeniable yearning to glut our senses with magnificent splendor and exquisite loveliness.

This is why thousands upon thousands of people flock to New England each October to feast their sights on the spectacular foliage. And why no one goes to West Texas to watch the tumbleweeds. Man is made for God. And because of that we are also made for beauty; for there is no Being more ravishingly and exquisitely beautiful than our triune God. We are created for a kind of beauty which only God is capable of splashing forth. The astonishing sunset, a harvest moon, crashing waves on a pristine beach, billowing clouds, flashing lightning, etc. are all God's gifts to man's sight, yet each of these are but elementary displays of His creative genius.

Jonathan Edwards wrote of this very thing in his own experience:

> *God's excellency, his wisdom, his purity and love, seemed to appear in everything: in the sun, moon, and stars; in the clouds, and blue sky; in the grass, flowers, trees; in the water, and all nature; which used greatly to fix my mind. I often used to sit and view the moon, for a long time; and so in the daytime, spent much time in viewing the clouds and sky, to behold the sweet glory of*

God in these things: in the meantime, singing forth with a low voice, my contemplations of the Creator and Redeemer. And scarce anything, among all the works of nature, was so sweet to me as thunder and lightning. Formerly, nothing had been so terrible to me. I used to be a person uncommonly terrified with thunder: and it used to strike me with terror, when I saw a thunderstorm rising. But now, on the contrary, it rejoiced me. I felt God at the first appearance of a thunderstorm. And used to take the opportunity at such times, to fix myself to view the clouds, and see the lightnings play, and hear the majestic and awful voice of God's thunder: which often times was exceeding entertaining, leading me to sweet contemplations of my great and glorious God.

Certainly we are not to go too far and become *worshippers* of nature. But Jonathan Edwards and a host of fragrant saints throughout the centuries would invite us to go far enough to at least bump the edge now and then. To ravish our God-given eyes and satiate our God-given spirits with the God-bestowed beauty He has drenched His universe with. Nothing else can get the job done. Not even Hollywood.

> **FLASHPOINT**
> Refuse to become familiar with your surroundings. There is always new beauty to behold.

No Greater Seductress

"Therefore, behold, I will allure her, will bring her into the wilderness, and speak comfort to her." Hosea 2:14

Priest and writer Brennan Manning tells the story of John Egan, an ordinary man whose journal was published not long after he died. In describing the journal Manning notes, *"It is the story of an ordinary man whose soul was seduced and ravished by Jesus Christ."* This is exactly what our Lord specializes in. Always has, always will. Just ask the prophet Hosea.

What a fascinating way to describe the means whereby God regains His wandering children! He *"allures"* them. He doesn't bully them, badger them, or force them. He simply allures them. In fact, this same Hebrew word is translated elsewhere as *"seduces"* (Ex.22:16). There is no greater seductress than God. He dangles His goodness in front of us, and then with a gleam in His eye He whispers into our ear, *"Oh, taste and see that the Lord is good; blessed is the man who trusts in Him."* (Ps.34:8) And this passage lets us know in no uncertain terms what it is about God that allures and seduces us away from this world's strong grasp upon us: *"the Lord is good."* It is the *goodness* of God, not the *judgment* of God, which most powerfully provokes deep repentance in our lives.

Here are some passages that emphasize this goodness:

Or do you despise the riches of His goodness, forbearance, and longsuffering, not knowing that the goodness of God leads you to repentance? Rom. 2:4

Afterward the children of Israel shall return and seek the LORD their God and David their king. They shall fear the LORD and His goodness in the latter days. Hosea 3:5

But when he came to himself, he said, 'How many of my father's hired servants have bread enough and to spare, and I perish with hunger! I will arise and go to my father... Lk. 15:17-18

For I know the thoughts that I think toward you, says the LORD, thoughts of peace and not of evil, to give you a future and a hope. Jer. 29:11

So I say it again. There is no greater seductress than our God. No kinder seductress. No purer seductress. No more alluring seductress. And, at the end of the day, no more satisfying seductress. Swiss Christian psychiatrist Paul Tournier put it so well:

...then suddenly there dawns upon us the vast, entire endowment of God's free love and forgiveness, and of the reconciliation He offers us in Jesus Christ. It is this which bowls us over, frees us from the burden of guilt, transforms us, and provokes 'metanoia.'

Metanoia is the Greek word for *"repentance."* Literally it means *"to change the mind."* And he is so, so right. It is the goodness of God—His *"free love and forgiveness"*—that catches our eye, dazzles our senses, captivates our hearts, and then causes us to change our minds about Who will take us home that night. And every night. And every day, too.

> **FLASHPOINT**
> The goodness of God is not merely a theological doctrine; it is most of all a relational magnet.

Genuine Christ-likeness

"My little children, for whom I labor in birth again until Christ is formed in you." Gal. 4:19

The goal of our ministry is not open for negotiation. God has decreed it in no uncertain terms—to cooperate with Him in helping others become more like His Son. As C.S. Lewis put it so well:

> *It is easy to think that the Church has a lot of different objects— education, building, missions, holding services....The Church exists for nothing else but to draw men into Christ, to make them*

little Christs. If they are not doing that, all the cathedrals, clergy, missions, sermons, even the Bible itself, are simply a waste of time. God became Man for no other purpose.

I'm struck, though, by how insipid the phrase *"becoming like Christ"* has become in our day. We think of Christlikeness in such safe, mellow, unthreatening terms that it would seem God is calling us to a life of little more than maxed-out niceness, a sort of kindness on steroids if you will. When we say God wants us to become like His Son, do we have any idea of how radical a proposition this is? The British Christian intellectual Dorothy Sayers puts it so well:

I believe it is a grave mistake to present Christianity as something charming and popular with no offense in it...We cannot blink the fact that Jesus meek and mild was so stiff in His opinions and so inflammatory in His language that He was thrown out of church, stoned, hunted from place to place, and finally gibbeted as a firebrand and a public danger. Whatever His peace was, it was not the peace of an amiable indifference...

The people who hanged Christ never, to do them justice, accused Him of being a bore—on the contrary, they thought Him too dynamic to be safe. It has been left for later generations to muffle up that shattering personality and surround Him with an atmosphere of tedium. We have very efficiently pared the claws of the Lion of Judah, certified Him 'meek and mild' and recommended Him as a fitting pet for pale curates and pious old ladies.

Those who knew Him, however...objected to Him as a dangerous firebrand.

Let us beware that we are not simply helping others become safer, cleaner, stiffer, and merely more biblically knowledgeable. God wants to use us to help them become 21st century firebrands, men and women through whom the Lion of Judah can go on the prowl again. Of course, it must first begin with us.

> **FLASHPOINT**
> Genuine Christ-likeness is the most radical undertaking known to man.

First-Hand Exposure

"They looked to Him and were radiant, and their faces were not ashamed." Ps.34:5

You cannot get a suntan by moonlight. Perhaps you never thought about that before but try it sometime. Go out some warm summer night when there is a clear sky and a full moon. Lay out under the moon with the full force of its light streaming down upon you. Stay there for a few hours. Then come inside and inspect yourself for any evidences of a newly acquired tan. No doubt, you will be disappointed.

Go out the next day and lay out in the open sun for a few hours. The result will be markedly different, I can assure you. Why? Very simple—it's the power of first-hand exposure. And the impotence of second-hand encounter.

As you're well aware, at night we are still getting sunlight. Only it's sunlight reflected by the moon to earth. The moon radiates no light of its own. During the day... ah, that's when we get first hand exposure to the original source. And it is only first hand exposure that changes the color of our skin. Or our spiritual lives.

Gifted teachers, outstanding preachers, or any of God's servants are at most only moons in God's order of things. The *best* they can do is simply reflect God's light and love to others around. And that is a wonderful and unspeakably high privilege. But only the true and living God can change a life. And only first hand exposure to Him can bring about that change. As David put it in Psalm 34, *"They looked to Him and were radiant, and their faces were not ashamed."* They didn't look to God's servants, they looked to *Him*. And that, my friend, makes all the difference.

Augustine wrote of his first hand exposure to God:

And what do I love when I love You? Not physical beauty...or the radiance of light that pleases the eye, or the sweet melody of old familiar songs, or the fragrance of flowers and ointments and spices... None of these do I love when I love my God.

Yet there is a kind of light, and a kind of melody, and a kind of fragrance, and a kind of food, and a kind of embracing when I love my God. They are the kind of light and sound and odor and food and love that affect the senses of the inner man.

...It hears melodies that never fade with time. It inhales lovely scents that are not blown away by the wind. It eats without diminishing or consuming the supply. It never gets separated from the embrace of God and never gets tired of it. That is what I love when I love my God.

Theologian John Wesley wrote, *"Here then I am, far from the busy ways of men. I sit down alone; only God is here. In his presence I open, I read his Book...and what I learn, I teach."* I love his phrase, *"only God is here."*

May I say it again—We cannot get a suntan by moonlight. Augustine couldn't. Wesley couldn't. David couldn't. And we can't. May God grant that we spend more time this year than ever before in pressing hard into the presence of the Original Source. Spiritual radiance and vitality can be found nowhere else.

FLASHPOINT
Only the Original Source can bring the change we need and the satisfaction we long for.

Christ-like Rudeness

"Then His disciples came and said unto Him, 'Do You know that the Pharisees were offended when they heard this saying?'" Matt.15:12

One of the characteristics I most admire about Jesus is His utter disregard for the approval of men. It is one of the things that made Him so free. So bold. And at times— so rude. Unapologetically rude. Certainly that's what His disciples discovered.

In Matt. 15 Christ has been exposing the hypocrisy of the scribes and Pharisees to their face:

> He answered and said to them, "Why do you also transgress the commandment of God because of your tradition?... Thus you have made the commandment of God of no effect by your tradition. Hypocrites! Well did Isaiah prophesy about you, saying: 'These people draw near to Me with their mouth, and honor Me with their lips, but their heart is far from Me. And in vain they worship Me, teaching as doctrines the commandments of men. Matt. 15:3-9

Christ's disciples recognized His words were offending these religious leaders, so they said to Him, *"Do You know that the Pharisees were offended when they heard this saying?"* (Matt. 15:12) His response? He kicked it into even higher gear. *"But He answered them and said, 'Every plant which My Heavenly Father has not planted will be uprooted. Let them alone.*

They are blind leaders of the blind. And if the blind leads the blind, both will fall into a ditch.'" (Matt. 15:13-14) My, oh my. Not exactly a Dale Carnegie response.

In "The Greatest Drama Ever Staged," Dorothy Sayers puts it so well:

> *To those who knew him…he in no way suggests a milk-and-water person; they objected to him as a dangerous firebrand. True, he was tender to the unfortunate, patient with honest inquirers, and humble before heaven; but he insulted respectable clergymen by calling them hypocrites. He referred to King Herod as 'that fox'; he went to parties in disreputable company and was looked upon as a 'gluttonous man and a winebibber, a friend of publicans and sinners'; he assaulted indignant tradesmen and threw them and their belongings out of the temple; he drove a coach-and-horses through a number of sacrosanct and hoary regulations; he cured diseases by any means that came handy, with a shocking casualness in the matter of other people's pigs and property; he showed no proper deference for wealth or social position; when confronted with neat dialectical traps, he displayed a paradoxical humour that affronted serious-minded people, and he retorted by asking disagreeably searching questions that could not be answered by rule of thumb.*

Jesus wouldn't have gone over too well down here in the South. He wouldn't have given into the social moorings which often keep straightforward truth-telling at a distance. Certainly He would not have been known for his gentlemanly charm or careful diplomacy. His startling kindness, yes. But not His careful maneuvering to keep others un-offended. He would just have loved as no other has loved. He would have moved forward into people's lives with an abandon and depth of concern that was unnerving. He would have cared so supremely for His Father's reputation that He undoubtedly would have alienated many in our present day church culture. And, at times, He would have been rude. But then again, rudeness is sometimes the most Christ-like response there is. Even in the South.

> **FLASHPOINT**
> Christ-likeness is not maxed-out niceness.
> It is fierce godliness.

Unintended Influence

"Now it was so, when Moses came down from Mount Sinai...that Moses did not know that the skin of his face shone while he talked with Him." Ex. 34:29

It was from J. Oswald Sanders that I first heard the term *"unconscious impression."* I've never forgotten the phrase or what he had to say about it. His point was simple, but profoundly powerful. Often the greatest influence we have on others is unintended, un-orchestrated, and wholly unrehearsed. It comes during those times when our defenses are down, when we've gone "off duty," and when we're oblivious to the fact that anyone is watching. Just like Moses, who *"did not know"* God's radiance was being reflected off of him.

It is at the most unguarded times that our naked spirituality is exposed most clearly, for better or worse. And it is in those times that the light of God-ward obedience shines most brightly. In 1871, a roving, atheistic journalist named Henry Stanley was hired to go down into Africa to do a story on the famous explorer and medical missionary David Livingstone. After finding Livingstone ten months later, he went on to discover something more, as he himself recounts:

> *For four months I lived with him in the same house or in the same boat or in the same tent, and I never found a fault in him. His gentleness never forsakes him. No harassing anxieties, distraction of mind, long separation from home and kindred, can make him complain. He thinks all will come out right at last; he has such faith in the goodness of Providence.*
>
> *I went to Africa as prejudiced as the biggest atheist in London. But there came for me a long time of reflection. I saw this solitary old man there and asked myself, 'How on earth does he stop here—is he cracked, or what? What inspires him?' For months*

after we met I found myself wondering at the old man carrying out all that was said in the Bible—'Leave all things and follow Me.' But little by little his sympathy for others became contagious, my sympathy was aroused, seeing his piety, his gentleness, his zeal, his earnestness, and how he went about his business, I was converted by him, although he had not tried to do it.

Later Stanley wrote, *"It wasn't Livingstone's preaching that converted me, it was his living."* Ah, the power of unconscious impression. How fragrant the life that sets its sights on enjoying and serving God regardless of the accolades or criticisms it draws from men! And how powerful as well.

FLASHPOINT
Spirituality is most powerfully expressed in the unguarded moments.

The Power of Supernatural Response

"But at midnight Paul and Silas were praying and singing hymns to God, and the prisoners were listening to them." Acts 16:25

A supernatural response preaches more loudly than a thousand sermons. John Wesley was once asked the secret to Methodism and how it had grown so rapidly. There were many things he could have pointed to—preaching, social good, education, small groups, etc. But he had one answer that trumped all of them. *"Our people die well"* was the number one reason he gave for their success. When the people of England saw their friends, family, and neighbors approach death in such a radically different manner than most, they began to take this thing called Christianity far more seriously. Such is the power of a supernatural response.

The fellow inmates of Paul and Silas began listening to them when they responded supernaturally. Eugene Peterson translates this verse in The Message beautifully, *"Along about midnight, Paul and Silas were at prayer and singing a robust hymn to God. The other prisoners couldn't believe their ears."* Prisoners don't sing praises to God at midnight unless there is something different about them. Something supernaturally different.

I well remember an incident from the early 1980's while I was a college pastor in College Station, Texas. Incoming freshman Bruce Goodrich was being initiated into the cadet corps at Texas A & M University. One early morning, he was forced to run until he dropped. Tragically, he never got up. Bruce Goodrich died at the very beginning of his first semester at A&M. The school, of course, prepared for the lawsuit which certainly the parents would bring against it. Unexpectedly, the lawsuit never came. But the following letter was sent by Bruce's father to the administration, faculty, student body, and the corps of cadets. It was published in the school newspaper—"The Battalion," and the city paper—"The Eagle."

I would like to take this opportunity to express the appreciation of my family for the great outpouring of concern and sympathy from Texas A & M University and the college community over the loss of our son Bruce. We were deeply touched by the tribute paid to him in The Battalion. We were particularly pleased to note that his Christian witness did not go unnoticed during his brief time on campus.

I hope it will be some comfort to know that we harbor no ill will in the matter. We know our God makes no mistakes. Bruce had an appointment with his Lord and is now secure in his celestial home. When the question is asked, 'Why did this happen?' perhaps one answer will be, 'So that many will consider where they will spend eternity.'

I say it again—a supernatural response preaches more loudly than a thousand sermons. Not that the thousand sermons don't have their place. But the best of sermons can still be quickly swept aside. Supernatural responses such as Mr. Goodrich's and his family make it more difficult to brush off the reality of a life-transforming God. Far, far more difficult.

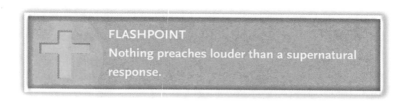

FLASHPOINT
Nothing preaches louder than a supernatural response.

Adorning the Doctrine of God

"Exhort bondservants to be obedient to their own masters, to be well pleasing in all things, not answering back, not pilfering, but showing all good fidelity, that they may adorn the doctrine of God our Savior in all things." Titus 2:9-10

Work matters. It matters much. But it's easy to lose sight of why it matters most. The most important thing about doing a great job is not the money it will bring in, the raise it may provide, the promotion it could lead to, or the recognition it likely will be given. Or even the personal satisfaction one derives from it. The most important thing about doing a great job is what it does for God. More specifically, His reputation. I love the way Paul puts it in this passage, *"that they may adorn the doctrine of God our Savior in all things."* The word Paul uses for "adorn" is literally the word we get *"cosmetics"* from. Eugene Peterson captures this original imagery beautifully in The Message, *"Then their good character will shine through their actions, adding luster to the teaching of our Savior God."*

I love that thought. We have the unspeakable privilege of *"adding luster"* to the word of God by simply doing a great job with a good attitude. Doing ordinary tasks extraordinarily well. Don't tell me that work is simply an unavoidable necessity. No, a thousand times, no! Our job is a stage, an arena, an individualized showcase for displaying the spectacularness of our God through our own handiwork. Dorothy Sayers has such a great word on this:

> *The Church's approach to an intelligent carpenter is usually confined to exhorting him not to be drunk and disorderly in his leisure hours, and to come to church on Sundays. What the Church should be telling him is this: that the very first demand that his religion makes upon him is that he should make good tables.*

> *Church by all means, and decent forms of amusement, certainly— but what use is all that if in the very center of his life and occupation he is insulting God with bad carpentry? No crooked table legs or ill-fitting drawers ever, I dare swear, came out of the carpenter's shop at Nazareth. Nor, if they did, could anyone*

believe that they were made by the same hand that made Heaven and earth. No piety in the worker will compensate for work that is not true to itself; for any work that is untrue to its own technique is a living lie...She (the Church) has forgotten that the secular vocation is sacred. Forgotten that a building must be good architecture before it can be a good church; that a painting must be well painted before it can be a good sacred picture; that work must be good work before it can call itself God's work.

I love her line, *"What the Church should be telling him is this: that the very first demand that his religion makes upon him is that he should make good tables."* I'm certain that Paul would have echoed a hearty amen to that. And so would his Carpenter Boss.

FLASHPOINT
Never underestimate the value of doing the ordinary extraordinarily well.

Fragrance
FIRE'S AROMA

*"Spirituality is not easy to define but its presence or absence
can easily be discerned. It has been called the diffused
fragrance which has been assimilated in the garden of the
Lord. It is the power to change the atmosphere by one's
presence, the unconscious influence which makes
Christ and spiritual things real to others."*

– J. OSWALD SANDERS –

*"Now thanks be to God who always leads us in triumph
in Christ, and through us diffuses the fragrance of His
knowledge in every place. For we are to God the fragrance
of Christ among those who are being saved and among those
who are perishing. To the one we are the aroma of death
leading to death, and to the other the aroma of life leading to
life. And who is sufficient for these things?"*

– II COR. 2:14-16 –

One of my fond memories of growing up was spending time each summer at our family cabin in the mountains of New Mexico. I especially loved waking up in the morning and smelling the fragrance of burning pine coming up from our downstairs fireplace. The sweet, crisp aroma beckoned me to come down the stairs and warm myself in front of the leaping flames.

True spirituality has an unmistakable, beckoning fragrance as well. I love J. Oswald Sanders' statement, "Spirituality is not easy to define but its presence or absence can easily be discerned. It has been called the diffused fragrance which has been assimilated in the garden of the Lord." These meditations are devoted to some of the more important ingredients necessary for this "diffused fragrance...assimilated in the garden of the Lord" to be imparted through our lives. A garden, which incidentally also includes thorns.

Right Kind of Obedience

"...so that we should serve in the newness of the Spirit and not in the oldness of the letter." Rom.7:6

It couldn't be any clearer. There is a kind of Christianity that is essentially Old Covenant spirituality—keeping God's commands in *"the oldness of the letter."* It is tired, musty, joyless, rule-driven, self-absorbed religiosity. And there is New Covenant spirituality—keeping God's commands in *"the newness of the Spirit."* The word for *"newness"* can just as easily be translated *"freshness."* I love that!

Vital obedience has the fresh scent of God upon it, for it is Spirit empowered, Christ-absorbed, and God-flaunting. And it is the only kind of obedience worth marketing to this darkened, skeptical world. As Paul puts it, *"Who also made us sufficient as ministers of the new covenant, not of the letter but of the Spirit; for the letter kills, but the Spirit gives life."* (II Cor. 3:6) I can't describe the difference between the two any better than Eugene Peterson:

The word Christian means different things to different people. To one person it means a stiff, uptight, inflexible way of life, colorless and unbending. To another it means a risky, surprised-filled venture, lived tiptoe at the edge of expectation.

Either of these pictures can be supported with evidence. There are numberless illustrations for either position in congregations all over the world. But if we restrict ourselves to biblical evidence, only the second image can be supported: the image of the person living zestfully, exploring every experience—pain and joy, enigma and insight, fulfillment and frustration—as a dimension of human freedom, searching through each for sense and grace. If we get our information from the biblical material, there is no doubt that the Christian life is a dancing, leaping, daring life.

How then does the other picture get painted in so many imaginations? How does anyone get the life of faith associated with dullness, with caution, with inhibition, with stodginess?...We might think that a people that has at the very heart of its common experience release from sin's guilt into the Spirit's freedom, a people who no longer lives under the tyranny of emotions or public opinion or bad memories, but freely in hope and in faith and in love—that these people would be critically alert to anyone or anything that would suppress their newly acquired spontaneity.

But in fact the community of faith, the very place where we are most likely to experience the free life, is also the very place where we are most in danger of losing it.

"Oldness of the letter"... "Newness of the Spirit"... Interesting that Paul doesn't give a third alternative—the mixture of the two. A kind of negotiated compromise between God's Spirit and our flesh, enabling us to keep our pride at least somewhat intact. No, apparently God sees it as one or the other. It's time we do the same.

Purpose-Driven Suffering

"But He knows the way I take; when He has tried me, I shall come forth as gold." Job 23:10

"But He knows...when He has tried me..." There is nothing random about our lives. Every trial, every heartache, every teardrop has to pass inspection by the Sovereign of the universe. A Sovereign Who holds His scepter with nail-pierced hands. As Jeremiah says *"For He does not afflict willingly nor grieve the children of men"* (Lam. 3:33). Though He does not afflict *"willingly,"* He does afflict certainly. And painfully. But it is purpose-driven suffering, with a perfect goal that is beyond what we are able to see many times. No—probably most of the time. C.S. Lewis puts it so well in *Mere Christianity:*

> *Imagine yourself as a living house. God comes in to rebuild that house. At first, perhaps, you can understand what He is doing.*

He is getting the drains right and stopping the leaks in the roof and so on: you knew that those jobs needed doing and so you are not surprised. But presently He starts knocking the house about in a way that hurts abominably and does not seem to make sense. What on earth is He up to? The explanation is that He is building quite a different house from the one you thought of—throwing out a new wing here, putting on an extra floor there, running up towers, making courtyards. You thought you were going to be made into a decent little cottage: but He is building a palace. He intends to come and live in it Himself.

Lewis also writes, *"Experience: that most brutal of teachers. But you learn, my God do you learn."*

How true! Left to myself I would settle for a cottage. Maybe you would to. Fortunately God does not leave any of us to our own insipid, pale, milk toast aspirations for spiritual growth. He takes us far beyond where we would ever choose to go on our own. And even though this taking is *"that most brutal of teachers"* and *"hurts abominably"* at times, it never hurts randomly. In some way, in some fashion, at some point, it always leads us to a spiritually wealthier place. Spurgeon wrote, *"The Lord gets His best soldiers out of the highlands of affliction."* No doubt that is true. Yet He does not allow His soldier to remain in those highlands one second longer than necessary. And in my book, that is no small matter.

> **FLASHPOINT**
> Every trial in our life must pass inspection.
> And it cannot last a second longer than
> absolutely necessary.

The Cost of Counting

Suffer hardship with me, as a good soldier of Jesus Christ."
II Tim.2:3

Hardship is fundamental to discipleship. Or, to put it another way, it costs to count. Too many times in my life I have lost sight of this. Or tried to dumb it down. But this passage in II Timothy is one of myriads reminding us that this present world far more resembles a battle field than an amusement park. That our primary goal in life cannot be what theologian Francis Schaeffer termed *"personal peace and affluency."* It is God-crafted, Christ-honoring, Spirit-empowered significance—whatever the cost.

A great example of the cost of significance is found in George Bernard Shaw's play, "Saint Joan"—the story of Joan of Arc. In Scene II there is an interchange between

Joan and King Charles as she urges him to summon the courage to fight for France. She promises him, *"I will put courage into thee."* To this he responds, *"But I don't want courage put into me. I want to sleep in a comfortable bed, and not live in continual terror of being killed or wounded. Put courage into the others, and let them have their bellyful of fighting; but let me alone."*

A few sentences later he says, *" I don't want to be any of these fine things you all have your heads full of: I want to be just what I am. Why can't you mind your own business, and let me mind mine?"*

To this she responds, *"Minding your own business is like minding your own body: it's the shortest way to make yourself sick. What is my business? Helping mother at home? What is thine? Petting lapdogs and sucking sugar-sticks? I call that muck. I tell thee it is God's business we are here to do: not our own."*

How well put! *"It is God's business we are here to do: not our own."* Christ Himself was gripped by this mighty calling:

For I have come down from heaven, not to do My own will, but the will of Him who sent Me. Jn. 6:38

My food is to do the will of Him who sent Me, and to finish His work. Jn. 4:34

I must work the works of Him who sent Me while it is day; the night is coming when no one can work. (Jn. 9:4) Truly, it is God's business we are here to do. He has given all of us something vitally unique to contribute to this world. There is a song only you can sing, a poem only you can write, a niche only you can fill, and an influence that you and you alone can exert. No one can step in and read your script for you, or serve as your understudy in life. Our short stay on this planet is meant to leave it a different and better place for the glory of God than when we came in. Inevitably though, it will require that we *"endure hardship...as a good soldier of Jesus Christ."* The other alternative is to stay at home, suck on sugar sticks, and pet lap dogs. And no believer can truly be satisfied with that.

FLASHPOINT
It costs to count. But it costs more not to.

Full Admission

"Then David said to Nathan, "I have sinned against the LORD." And Nathan said to David, "The LORD also has taken away your sin; you shall not die." II Sam.12:13

One of the most important ingredients of godliness is sincere fault admission. To refuse to divert blame onto any other source and to take complete responsibility for our own failure is one of the most humbling enterprises known to man—and one of the most powerful. By it David became the man that Saul could have been. When David was confronted with his sin his response was full ownership—*"I have sinned against the Lord."* No justifications ("she was so beautiful"), no rationalizations ("It's not that big a thing. After all I'm the king."), no blame shifting ("she shouldn't have been bathing in the open"). Just complete responsibility for the sin *he* had committed through no one else's fault but his own.

When Saul was confronted with his sin he had a very different response. *"When I saw that the people were scattered from me, and that you did not come within the days appointed, and that the Philistines gathered together at Michmash, then I said, 'The Philistines will now come down on me at Gilgal, and I have not made supplication to the LORD.' Therefore I felt compelled, and offered a burnt offering."* (I Sam. 13:11-12.) Note the plethora of reasons behind his sin. But in the final analysis, Saul valued his own ego and other's opinion of him far more than humble integrity before God and men. Confession that is pockmarked with justifications is no confession at all.

The same holds true in our relationships with others, especially loved ones. I heard recently about a group of teenagers sitting around a campfire on a youth camping trip. The leader of the trip posed the question, "What do you most appreciate about your father?" There were many different answers such as his hard work for the family, the time he spent with his children, the fun they had with him, etc. Then one young man ventured, "What I most appreciate about my dad is that he is willing to admit to us when he was wrong in the way he handled a situation." Apparently there was dead silence until one girl chimed in, "I would give anything for my dad to do that." Almost every other teenager there said the same thing in one way or another. The group leader told me that the teenagers later kept telling that one young man that he had no idea how lucky he was to have a father that would do that.

Israeli Prime Minister Disraeli was exactly right when he said, *"One of the hardest things in this world is to admit you are wrong. And nothing is more helpful in resolving a situation than its frank admission."* Sincerely uttering the simple words "I was wrong" is often times one of the most difficult things a person can do—and most courageous and most powerful. This holds true whether it be at the workplace or in politics or ministry or with our family. Especially with our family.

> **FLASHPOINT**
> Full admission of fault is one of the most humbling enterprises in the world—and most powerful.

"Kindling for the Fire"

"Who makes...His ministers a flame of fire." Ps. 104:4

Amy Carmichael ministered for fifty-five years in India, rescuing countless young girls from a life of forced prostitution. In addition to her ministry to India's outcasts, she wrote thirty-six books and influenced multitudes of young men and women to venture forth into the unreached mission fields of the world. A prolific writer, her words are memorable. Some of her gems were these quotes:

The only expenditure, and all its outworkings, for which God can be held to be responsible is that which He directs.

It is a safe thing to trust Him to fulfill the desires which He creates.

You can give without loving, but you cannot love without giving.

But perhaps most famous of all is this poem:

> *From prayer that asks that I may be*
> *Sheltered from winds that beat on Thee,*
> *From fearing when I should aspire,*
> *From faltering when I should climb higher*
> *From silken self, O Captain, free*
> *Thy soldier who would follow Thee.*
> *From subtle love of softening things,*

From easy choices, weakenings,
(Not thus are spirits fortified,
Not this way went the Crucified)
From all that dims Thy Calvary
O Lamb of God, deliver me.

Give me the love that leads the way,
The faith that nothing can dismay
The hope no disappointments tire,
The passion that will burn like fire;
Let me not sink to be a clod;
Make me Thy fuel, Flame of God.

Not surprisingly, the poem is entitled *"Flame of God."*

May God grant that we each increasingly fulfill our highest calling on earth—to yield ourselves up as kindling for the Fire. The Fire of God that is. There simply is no greater use of a life, no greater joy in a heart, no greater good to our fellow man, and no greater glory to our risen Savior than to be God's torch in this darkened world. Thank you Amy for helping show us the way.

FLASHPOINT
Make us Thy fuel, O Flame of God.

Heart Transplants

"Then I will give them a heart to know Me, that I am the LORD..." Jer. 24:7

"...but I will put My fear in their hearts so that they will not depart from Me." Jer. 32:40

One of the wondrous realities of the New Covenant is that God has given us new hearts which yearn for what matters most in the universe—God. Nothing matters more than God. Nothing satisfies more than God. Nothing terrifies more than God. Nothing thrills more than God. And this new, divinely implanted yearning transforms what is our rightful obligation into what is our innate enjoyment. Notice the promise—*"I will give...I will put."* This new inclination toward God is not the result of trying harder or praying longer; but wholly the gifting of indwelling deity. In the words of Dante, we have become *"ingodded."*

Jonathan Edwards writes, *The first effect of the power of God in the heart in regeneration is to give the heart a divine taste or sense; to cause it to have a relish of the loveliness and sweetness of the supreme excellency of the divine nature.*

Martin Luther puts it thus in his commentary on Galatians:

> *The Holy Ghost is sent forth into the hearts of the believers...*
> *This sending is accomplished by the preaching of the Gospel*
> *through which the Holy Spirit inspires us with fervor and light,*
> *with new judgment, new desires, and new motives. This happy*

innovation is not a derivative of reason or personal development, but solely the gift and operation of the Holy Ghost.

What a great phrase—*"happy innovation!"* Deeper than our sin, deeper than our pain, deeper than our fear is something clean, pure, and godly within us that ceaselessly yearns to know and reflect God. We can do His will not only because it is good for us, but because it delights the taste buds of our new nature. The desire to do the will of God isn't something we have to work up, but something to fall back on. Not that it's always easy. But it is always available. And if that isn't good news, I'm not sure what is.

God has made His glory and our satisfaction to be synchronized with one another. In other words, our longing for personal satisfaction and God's resolve for personal glorification are not opposed to one another as is so often supposed. We will find ourselves most deeply satisfied and invigorated when we are most dominated and intoxicated by God and His glory. It is the greatest win-win situation known to man. Jonathan Edwards writes, *"God's respect to the creature's good, and His respect to Himself, is not a divided respect; but both are united in one, as the happiness of the creature… is happiness in union with Himself."*

Ah, what an amazing proposition! Radical, wholly abandoned, white-hot pursuit of the living God is simply doing what we were made to do. And doing what we were made *to want* to do. And doing what we were made to enjoy above all else. Obedience therefore—in the final analysis—is simply the glutting of our new nature!

> **FLASHPOINT**
> The glory of God is not simply our calling;
> it is also our delight. All thanks to a heart
> transplant from on high.

Expanding Our Borders of Gratitude

"But I will hope continually, and will praise You yet more and more." Ps.71:14

Notice the psalmist doesn't say that he will praise God *"yet more and more"* if God provides enough material in his life to be worthy of praise. Rather, he says he *"will hope continually."* Ongoing hope can never be rooted in the circumstances of life, for they are too fickle and variable to warrant such hope. Only an eternally kind, unchanging God is worthy of such confidence. Not only on Thanksgiving, but every other day of the year as well.

Few things will more quickly upgrade the quality of our lives or the increase the glory that we bring to God than expanding the borders of our gratitude. What I mean by this is cultivating the ability to genuinely give thanks for those things we normally take for granted, or finding new avenues of gratitude for things we have never seen before.

It means repenting of the spirit of entitlement which plagues all of us and pushing forward our praise and thanksgiving into domains we don't often think to go. Like having a roof over our head. Like having air-conditioning or heating. Like having food on the table (for most of us, more than enough food). Like having a car. Like being able to read. Like being able to hear. Like being able to walk. On and on it goes. And most of all, for being on our way to heaven with sins forgiven because of the blood of the perfect, spotless Lamb of God. As the psalmist put it:

Bless the LORD, O my soul; and all that is within me, bless His holy name! Bless the LORD, o my soul, and forget not all His benefits: Who forgives all your iniquities, Who heals all your diseases, Who redeems your life from destruction, Who crowns you with loving kindness and tender mercies, Who satisfies your mouth with good things, so that your youth is renewed like the eagle's…

He has not dealt with us according to our sins, nor punished us according to our iniquities. For as the heavens are high above the earth, so great is His mercy toward those who fear Him; as far as the east is from the west, so far has He removed our transgressions from us. As a father pities his children, so the LORD pities those who fear Him. For He knows our frame; He remembers that we are dust. Ps. 103:1-5,10-14

Matthew Henry was a great bible expositor and English clergyman who lived from 1662 to 1714. Once he was robbed while out on horseback. That night he wrote in his journal, *"I thank Thee first because I was never robbed before; second, because although they took my purse they did not take my life; third, because although they took my all, it was not much; and fourth because it was I who was robbed, and not I who robbed."* That, my friend, is what I mean by expanding the borders of our gratitude. May we each follow in his footsteps!

> **FLASHPOINT**
> Life is a feast for the grateful. There is always something to be thankful for.

Supernatural Influence

"...the Son can do nothing of Himself" Jn.5:19

"...the Father Who dwells in Me does the works." Jn.14:10

Who are supernatural influencers? Simply put, they are men and women living in vital communion with God, desperately depending upon His resources, and yielded to

His flow through their lives. They are not trying to make something happen for Christ; they are jealous to see that what escapes from their lives is something He has caused to happen. They may or may not have formal theological training or great intellectual abilities. They may or may not have charismatic personalities or natural leadership abilities. They may or may not have high standing in society; be it sports, acting, politics, etc. God is neither bound nor impressed by any of these things. What they have is brokenness of spirit and confidence in Christ that He alone will do through them whatever the need of the moment requires. J. Oswald Sanders puts it well:

> *The spiritual leader, however, influences others not by the power of his own personality alone but by that personality irradiated, interpenetrated, and empowered by the Holy Spirit. Because he permits the Holy Spirit undisputed control in his life, the Spirit's power can flow unhindered through him to others.*

Christ's entire life was a fragrant testimony to the power of undisputed neediness. "The Son can do nothing of Himself" (Jn.5:19) and *"I can do nothing of Myself"* (Jn.5:30) are but a few examples of the kind of radical distrust Christ had in His own native abilities. What then was the secret to the most dynamic Life ever lived on this earth? Christ Himself gives the answer: *"the Father Who dwells in Me does the works."* (Jn.14:10) Christ lived the most dynamic life ever lived because He lived the most dependent life ever lived. And He calls us to the same.

Yet it is so hard for us to fully yield to this truth. Our flesh desperately wants part of the action. It yearns to get at least some credit for the good in our lives. It pleads to stay in at least partial control and violently protests the terrifying prospect of relying only on God. C.S. Lewis is exactly right in his observation that our problem is not in trusting God. It is in trusting God *alone*.

But the reality is that true spiritual influence requires as radical a dependency on Christ's indwelling life for service as it did on Christ's shed blood for justification. Jonathan Edwards put it like this: *"There is an absolute and universal dependence of the redeemed on God. The nature and contrivance of our redemption is such, that the redeemed are in every thing directly, immediately, and entirely dependent on God: they are dependent on Him for all, and are dependent on Him every way."* This comes from my favorite work of his, "God Glorified in Man's Dependency." Bottom line—handiwork worthy of the name of God can only be done by God. May our lives increasingly reflect this great truth.

Is there not something within you my friend, rising up from your heart, which yearns to know that your life has been part of something that required God? Of course there is. Nothing on the face of the earth compares with the deep thrill and indescribable satisfaction of knowing, but knowing, that we have been part of something that can only be accredited to supernatural intervention. May He grant that this happen more and more for all of us.

FLASHPOINT
Busyness requires nothing of God. Effectiveness requires everything.

The Fire Triangle

FIRE'S TRIUMVIRATE

Triumvirate
*any joint rule by three men,
a board of three officials jointly
responsible for some task.*

F*ire has its own triumvirate. It's called the "fire triangle." It is not possible to have a fire without the three strongmen: oxygen, fuel, and heat. Without sufficient heat, a fire cannot begin, and it cannot continue. Without fuel, a fire will stop.Without sufficient oxygen, a fire cannot begin, and it cannot continue. Simply put, there is no possibility of sustained fire without all three of these elements making their essential and unique contribution.*

Likewise, Christianity has its own "fire triangle," a spiritual triumvirate if you will. "And now abide faith, hope, love, these three…" *writes the apostle Paul in I Cor. 13:13. In fact, Paul continuously used these three virtues as the measuring stick for determining the spiritual health of the churches he addressed in his letters:*

"remembering without ceasing your work of faith, labor of love, and patience of hope in our Lord Jesus Christ in the sight of our God and Father," I Thess. 1:3,9-10

"since we heard of your faith in Christ Jesus and of your love for all the saints; because of the hope which is laid up for you in heaven…" Col. 1:4-5 *See also* Heb. 10:22-24

It is faith that gives entrance *into the Christian life; it is love that gives* effectiveness *in the Christian life, and it is hope that gives* endurance *throughout the Christian life. These meditations are devoted to this divine triumvirate.*

Longing For Home

"For I am hard pressed between the two, having a desire to depart and be with Christ, which is far better." Phil.1:23

Every believer is an eternal spirit trapped between two worlds. One world beckons us home to eternal rest and unimaginable joy. The other calls us forth to spiritual battle, heartache, exhaustion, and periodic tastes of the presence and power of God. Some days more, other days less. Who wouldn't want to go home?

The older I get, the more convinced I am that the Christian life—properly lived—deepens homesickness. This world truly far more resembles a battlefield than an amusement park. As the hymn says,*"This world is not my home, I'm just a passing through."* Paul puts it even more passionately, describing the feeling as *"having a desire to depart and be with Christ."* The word he uses for *"desire"* (epithumia) is normally translated *"lust."* We find here one of the lusts of a godly man's heart—to go home and finally be in perfect union with the Lord. Famed British author and journalist Malcolm Muggeridge said at age 79 in "The Great Liberal Death Wish."

I feel so strongly at the end of my life that nothing can happen to us in any circumstances that is not part of God's purpose for us. Therefore, we have nothing to fear, nothing to worry about, except that we should rebel against His purpose, that we should fail to detect it and fail to establish some sort of relationship with Him and His divine will. On that basis, there can be no black despair, no throwing in of our hand…

You know, it's a funny thing, but when you're old, as I am, there are all sorts of extremely pleasant things that happen to you. One of them is, you realize that history is nonsense, but I won't go into that now. The pleasantest thing of all is that you wake up in the night at about, say, three a.m., and you find that you are half in and half out of your battered old carcass. And it seems quite a toss-up whether you go back and resume full occupancy of your mortal body, or make off toward the bright glow you see in the sky, the lights of the City of God. In this limbo between life and death, you know beyond any shadow of doubt that, as an infinitesimal particle of God's creation, you are a participant in God's purpose for His creation, and that that purpose is loving and not hating, is creative and not destructive, is everlasting and not temporal, is universal and not particular. With this certainty comes an extraordinary sense of comfort and joy.

Then he ended his address with these words, *"The essential feature, and necessity of life is to know reality, which means knowing God. Otherwise our mortal existence is, as Saint Teresa of Avila said, no more than a night in a second—class hotel."*

Eight years later Muggeridge saw those lights firsthand. And he departed from this *"second-class hotel"* called earth. But the homesickness never left him during those remaining years, nor should ours.

> **FLASHPOINT**
> Homesickness is one of the clearest
> indicators of the vitality of our faith.

The Absurdity of Faith

"By faith Abraham obeyed when he was called to go out to the place which he would afterward receive as an inheritance. And he went out, not knowing where he was going."
Heb. 11:8

A catheter into the human heart? Absolutely absurd. At least this was the opinion of everyone in Werner Forssman's world in the late 1920's. While inserting a catheter into the bladder was common practice, no one,—but no one—believed the human heart could withstand such an invasion. No one but Werner himself.

So one morning in 1929 Werner went into the hospital where he worked, tied his lab assistant to a table to prevent interference, inserted a catheter into his arm, and ran it all the way into the right atrium of his heart. He then walked up three stories to have himself x-rayed. The rest, as they say, is history. Werner Forssman had paved the way for heart catheterization.

In 1956 he was awarded the Nobel Prize for his efforts and contribution to medicine. In talking about his daring attempt in 1929, he noted, *"One cannot achieve the impossible without attempting the absurd."*

It strikes me that this is a great description of the kind of faith that makes a lasting difference in this fallen world. *Absurd.*

Absurd that Noah would build an ark when it had not rained.

Absurd that Abraham would leave Ur of the Chaldees for a land he would only recognize once he got there...if he got there.

Absurd that Moses would turn his back on all that Egypt offered to wander in the Sinai with rebellious Israelites.

Absurd that Peter would get out of a boat to walk on water.

Absurd that David would dare to take on a giant named Goliath.

Absurd, absurd, absurd... but truly it is the only way that God unleashes His power before a skeptical world. And the greatest absurdity? That God uses you and me to get His work done. Work that really should only be done by angels. Now *that* is truly absurd! Wonderfully absurd.

> **FLASHPOINT**
> The faith that makes the biggest difference is almost always labeled absurd.

Rivers of Blessing

"If you extend your soul to the hungry and satisfy the afflicted soul, then your light shall dawn in the darkness, and your darkness shall be as the noonday. The Lord will guide you continually, and satisfy your soul in drought, and strengthen your bones; you shall be like a watered garden, and like a spring of water, whose waters do not fail." Is.58:10-11

The life of Christ relentlessly pushes forward for expression within every believer. The only question is how we will respond to this supernaturally bestowed restlessness. We can either open our floodgates wide or keep them tightly shut. One choice results in spiritual vitality. The other, spiritual stagnation. Bruce Fairchild Barton put it so well:

There are two seas in Palestine.

One is fresh, and fish are in it. Splashes of green adorn its banks. Trees spread their branches over it and stretch out their thirsty roots to sip of its healing waters. Along its shores the children play as children played when He was there. He loved it. He could look across its silver surface when He spoke His parables.

And on a rolling plain not far away He fed five thousand people. The river Jordan makes this sea with sparkling water from the hills. So it laughs in the sunshine. And men build their houses near to it, and birds their nests; and every kind of life is happier because it is there.

The river Jordan flows on south into another sea. Here no splash of fish, no fluttering of leaf, no song of birds, no children's laughter. Travelers choose another route, unless on urgent business. The air hangs heavy above its water, and neither man nor beast nor fowl will drink.

What makes this mighty difference in these neighbor seas? Not the river Jordan. It empties the same good water into both. Not the soil in which they lie; not the country round about.

This is the difference. The Sea of Galilee receives but does not keep the Jordan. For every drop that flows into it another drop flows out. The giving and receiving go on in equal measure.

The other sea is shrewder, hoarding its income jealously. It will not be tempted into any generous impulse. Every drop it gets, it keeps.

The Sea of Galilee gives and lives. The other sea gives nothing. It is named The Dead.

There are two kinds of people in the world. There are two seas in Palestine.

What a great description of people's lives! Dead Sea people are *shrewder, hoarding their income jealously. They will not be tempted into any generous impulse. Every drop they get, they keep.* Sea of Galilee people *receive but do not keep the blessings. For every drop that flows into them another drop flows out. The giving and receiving go on in equal measure.* Enough said.

> **FLASHPOINT**
> Be imitators of the Sea of Galilee.
> Drink deeply, flow freely.

In the Nick of Time

"So it shall be, when you are on the verge of battle, that the priest shall approach and speak to the people." Deut. 20:2

Ever notice that the Lord never seems to show up too soon? That it is not until we are *"on the verge"* of moving forward in His will for us that He sends His enablement and provisions? The Israelites weren't blessed with the priest's presence and words until they were right on the brink of battle. Then, and only then, did the priest show up. And so it is with us.

We are encouraged by the writer of Hebrews, *"Let us therefore come boldly to the throne of grace, that we may obtain mercy and find grace to help in time of need."* (Heb. 4:16) According to eminent Greek scholar A.T. Robertson, the phrase *"help in time of need"* means essentially *"just in the nick of time."* I love that thought—God's enabling grace is given to us "just in the nick of time". How true!

God does not Fed-Ex His enabling grace ahead of time to alleviate the fear and risk-taking of faith. The waters of Jordan did not recede until the priests bearing the ark actually put their feet into the river (Josh. 3:13-17). The wall of Jericho showed no cracks on the first six days. It was only after they took the risk to walk around the wall the complete number of times decreed by God that *"the wall fell down flat."* (Josh.6:20). God *does* show up in response to believing obedience. But rarely, if ever, as early on as we would like.

Holocaust survivor and writer Corrie ten Boom tells a wonderful story of how her father helped her learn this lesson of God's timing in providing for her. He reminded her that when she was a very little girl they often used to ride the bus together. Then he asked her, *"When did I give you the bus token?"* She responded, *"Just as I was stepping onto the bus."* To which he responded, *"And so it is with our heavenly Father. He will provide for our needs and He will strengthen. But usually not until we are stepping onto the bus...until we are moving forward into His calling on our lives."* And God provided that grace and strength for her throughout her years in the Nazi prison camps. And God will do the same for us. Not ahead of time, but always *in the nick of time.*

FLASHPOINT
God's timing in showing up is perfect.

God's Viewpoint

"But when He saw the multitudes, He was moved with compassion for them, because they were weary and scattered, like sheep having no shepherd." Mtt.9:36

Not long ago I had the great privilege of hearing Brother Andrew, founder of Open Doors ministries, speak at our church. God used him to absolutely rock my world concerning how I view Muslims, especially terrorist organizations. Among the many penetrating things he said was this—God does not look down at humanity and see people as members of Al Qaeda, Hamas, Hezbollah, or any terrorist group. Nor as Democrat, Republican, or Tea Party. He doesn't see us as black, white, yellow, or brown, as male or female, American or other nationality, gay or straight, white collar or blue collar. And God does not view humanity as Muslim, Jew, Buddhist, Hindu, Animist, or any other religious distinction.

When God looks out on mankind, He sees them primarily as scattered sheep. *"But when He saw the multitudes, He was moved with compassion for them, because they were weary and scattered, like sheep having no shepherd."* In other words, Christ sees every person as a precious individual for whom He came and died. Pure and simple. And people have either received His unspeakable gift or they haven't. Pure and simple. And that's His primary vantage point on humanity. Pure and simple.

Brother Andrew then went on to describe some of the meetings he has had with high ranking leaders in several terrorist organizations and the hunger so many of them had to hear the gospel of Christ. He told us that like everyone else, they are simply *"sheep without a shepherd."* At least that's how our Lord sees them.

He concluded by asking how many of us had prayed for Muslim terrorists that morning? That month? That year?

Ever? He wasn't asking for a show of hands, which was fortunate, because I—like most I'm sure—would not have been able to raise mine. To my shame.

So this morning I prayed for the leadership of Al Qaeda for the first time in my life. And for the first time I thought of them first and foremost as those for whom Christ died. And that I needed just as much of Christ's blood as any of them. And it felt like the most Christian prayer I have prayed in a long time.

Canon Frederic William Farrar, the 19th century Dean of Canterbury put it so well:

Each human soul is like a cavern full of gems. The casual observer glances into it through some cranny, and all looks dark and sullen and useless. But let light enter into it and lo! It will flash with crystals and amethysts and quiver under the touch of brightness. If souls do not shine before you it is because you bring them no light to make them shine. Throw away your miserable, smouldering, fuming torch of conceit and hatred, lift up to them the light of love, and lo! They will arise and shine; yea, flame and burn with an undreamt of glory.

> **FLASHPOINT**
> May God grant that we throw away our smoldering torch of conceit and see people as Christ sees them—sheep without a shepherd.

Spellbound Living

"...looking for the blessed hope and glorious appearing of our great God and Savior Jesus Christ" Titus 2:13

John Wesley was once visiting with a wealthy Englishman who was also a strong believer. As this man showed Wesley around his large estate, they enjoyed several hours of rich fellowship. Toward the end of the time Wesley commented on what a wonderful home and grounds God had blessed this man with. He then confided, "I too have a relish for these things." And then with a distant look in his eye, he remarked, "But, there is another world."

Another world. It would seem that God's choice servants are inevitably gripped by this great reality. And it is why they go through their days in this world with their hearts residing in another world, the coming world. And it is why homesickness is part and parcel of godly living. It is also the foundation for an eternal perspective. An eternal perspective is what happens in believers' lives when *what presently is* becomes inseparably merged with *what ultimately will be.* It is the ability to continually see beyond the temporal to the eternal, and thus live in the immediate in light of the ultimate. It is the cultivated art of being able to see past the delights and difficulties of this present age to the glorious and unfading realities of another day, another kingdom, another home, and another treasure. In a word, it is the *"long look"* of life. And it is the basis for every pilgrim's homesickness. To put it another way, life is meant to be lived spellbound. Spellbound by another time, another place, another existence—i.e. *"the blessed hope and glorious appearing of our great God and Savior Jesus Christ."* The word translated *"looking for"* is much better rendered *"eagerly awaiting."* The believer is called to live with his feet planted in this world while his heart is held captive by the next. Some see this as mere escapism or being *"so heavenly minded that one is of no earthly good."* C.S. Lewis has a great word on this:

> *Hope is one of the Theological virtues. This means that a continual looking forward to the eternal world is not (as some modern people think) a form of escapism or wishful thinking, but one of the things a Christian is meant to do. It does not mean that we are to leave the present world as it is. If you read history you will find that the Christians who did most for the present world were just those who thought most of the next. The Apostles themselves, who set on foot the conversion of the Roman Empire, the great men who built up the Middle Ages, the English Evangelicals who abolished the Slave Trade, all left their mark on Earth, precisely because their minds were occupied with Heaven. It is since Christians have largely ceased to think of the other world that they have become so ineffective in this. Aim at Heaven and you will get earth "thrown in": aim at earth and you will get neither.*

This eternal perspective is a very large reason why Wesley averaged three sermons a day for fifty-four years (over 40,000 sermons in all), covered more than 250,000 miles by horseback or carriage, published over 5,000 tracts, pamphlets, and books, and proclaimed the gospel to hundreds of thousands throughout England. It is why countless saints throughout the ages have stayed the course and spent their few days on commodities which will last forever. May God grant that we be numbered among them.

FLASHPOINT
The long look and the significant life walk hand in hand.

Cosmic Perspective

"Lift up your eyes to the heavens, and look on the earth beneath. For the heavens will vanish away like smoke, the earth will grow old like a garment, and those who dwell in it will die in like manner; but My salvation will be forever, and My righteousness will not be abolished." Is. 51:6

"Congregations are not just places to be reminded of what one ought to do. They are spaces where 'ought' is put in cosmic perspective," writes sociologist Nancy Tatom Ammerman. I love that thought and her phrase *"cosmic perspective."* Church is

not simply the place that we are to be reminded of our moral and spiritual duties. It is the place that we are reminded of how titanically high the stakes are in this thing called life and the critical importance of eternal perspective. We all desperately need the "long look" of life and history. That cosmic perspective where all of existence bows at the throne of God and takes on its rightful subservient dimensions. What a great passage we find here for this very thing! God beckons us to lift up our eyes and gaze upon everything we can see in the present—*"the heavens... the earth...and those who dwell in it."* Take a good, hard look at each of these. God created them; they display His unrivaled touch and fashioning. They are not just good, they are very good.

But God wants us to know something very important about each of these great wonders. Something that should radically and unalterably affect the direction of our lives. Something that should keep us from becoming overly impressed by any of these wonders. And it is simply this: None of them are going to last. The present heavens will be reduced to a wisp of smoke, fading away before the new heavens (II Pet. 3:10-13). The present earth will be tossed aside like an old, stained t-shirt, replaced by a new earth. And the inhabitants of earth? Well, as George Bernard Shaw quipped, *"The statistics on death are impressive; one out of one."* Everyone will return to the dust from which they were taken. What then, is going to last?

Ah, that is God's point in this passage. His *"salvation"* and His *"righteousness"* will endure throughout the ages.

They will never become outdated or tarnished or obsolete. And God gives us but a few short days on this planet to traffic in these very things. These are unspeakably precious commodities. Eternal commodities. Never-to-be-regretted-of commodities. And if our lives are going to count for things of eternal consequence, they must, *they must,* in some form or fashion be seasoned with His divine salvation and His supernatural righteousness. Not just experienced by us, but also given away through us.

What could matter more? What higher calling for a mortal could there be? Frail, finite, stick-'em-and-they-bleed, flawed people like you and me handling things of such eternal consequence that they really should only be entrusted to angels. But for some crazy, yet wonderful reason, God has placed them within our grasp, our reach, and our life calling. May we never recover from this cosmic perspective. Or ever settle for less than abandoning ourselves to the high adventure of being men and women through whom the eternal commodities spill over into this temporal world. And especially, its temporary residents. Tell me, please tell me, what else are you going to do with your life bigger than that?

FLASHPOINT
We cannot do anything bigger with our lives than channel the things of eternity.

Our Sojourn

"By faith he sojourned in the land of promise, as in a strange country...For he looked for a city which hath foundations, whose builder and maker is God." Heb.11:9-10

"Beloved, I beg you as sojourners and pilgrims, abstain from fleshly lusts which war against the soul," I Pet. 2:11

The word *"sojourn"* ultimately comes from two Latin words which literally mean to *"be under a day"* or *"spend a day."* I love that thought. Truly this life is but a day at best; a wisp of smoke against eternity's skyline. As James asks,*"For what is your life? Is not even a vapor...?"* (Jas.4:14) No wonder we are called sojourners in this world and citizens in the next.

I highly recommend to you Jonathan Edwards' short treatise entitled "The Christian Pilgrim." In it he writes,

A traveler is not wont to rest in what he meets with, however comfortable and pleasing, on the road. If he passes through pleasant places, flowery meadows, or shady groves, he does not take up his content in these things, but only takes a transient view of them as he goes along. He is not enticed by fine appearances to put off the thought of proceeding. No, but his journey's end is in his mind.

If he meets with comfortable accommodations at an inn, he entertains no thoughts of settling there. He considers that these things

are not his own, that he is but a stranger, and when he has refreshed himself, or tarried for a night, he is for going forward. And it is pleasant to him to think that so much of the way is gone.

I love his thought, *"If he meets with comfortable accommodations at an inn, he entertains no thoughts of settling there."* As C.S. Lewis put it, "Our Father refreshes us on the journey with some pleasant inns, but will not encourage us to mistake them for home."

Thank God this world is not our home; *"We're just a passing through"* as the old hymn puts it. Yet how desperately easy it is for all of us to hang on to this age's pleasures and treasures as if they were our final stop. But the reality is that this world—at its absolute best—is a Motel 6. Sometimes a very nice Motel 6. But a Motel 6 nonetheless. The Ritz Carlton is not until the next life...so let's keep moving.

FLASHPOINT
Enjoy the good things in life...with a loose grip.

4

Firewood

FIRE'S COMMUNITY

"When I first became a Christian, about fourteen years ago, I thought I could do it on my own, by retiring to my rooms and reading theology, and I wouldn't go to the churches and gospel halls. I disliked very much their hymns, which I considered to be fifth-rate poems set to sixth-rate music. But as I went on I saw the great merit of it. I came up against different people of quite different outlooks and different education, and then gradually my conceit just began peeling off.

I realized that the hymns (which were just sixth-rate music) were, nevertheless, being sung with devotion and benefit by an old saint in elastic-side boots in the opposite pew, and then you realize that you aren't fit to clean those boots. It gets you out of your solitary conceit".

– C.S. LEWIS –

Lewis discovered what every Christian must embrace sooner or later. We need more logs than just ourselves. An isolated log will burn out far more quickly than one which is joined together with other logs. And so will the believer. His statement, "I thought I could do it on my own" is the certain path to one's fire becoming quickly extinguished. King Solomon puts it so well, "Two are better than one, because they have a good reward for their labor. For if they fall, one will lift up his companion. But woe to him who is alone when he falls, for he has no one to help him up. Again, if two lie down together, they will keep warm; but how can one be warm alone? Though one may be overpowered by another, two can withstand him. And a threefold cord is not easily broken." *Ecc. 4:9-12.*

These meditations are devoted to the vital importance of Christian community and the heart attitudes essential for its success.

Living Arm in Arm

"Two are better than one, because they have a good reward for their labor. For if they fall, one will lift up his companion. But woe to him who is alone when he falls, for he has no one to help him up." Solomon Ecc.4:9-12

Those who were there still talk about it. It happened years ago at the Seattle Special Olympics, a competition for physically and mentally handicapped children. The hundred-yard dash had nine entrants. The gun sounded and the runners started out as fast as they were able. Then one little boy tripped, fell on the track, and began to cry. The other eight heard his cry and all stopped to turn and look. Seeing him on the ground, they walked back to him— every one of them.

One little girl with Down syndrome bent down, kissed his leg, and said, "This will make it feel better." Then all nine put their arms around one another and walked together to the finish line. Everyone in the stadium stood and applauded, their cheers continuing for several minutes.

Even as I write this I find myself internally stirred. What is it about this true story that touches something deep within and brings a stadium full of people to their feet? Maybe it awakens our intuitive sense that we cannot live life on our own. It reminds us that we all need others in our life to dust us off, to help us to our feet, and walk arm in arm with us towards the finishing line of life. This is exactly what King Solomon was referring to when he wrote,

Two are better than one, because they have a good reward for their labor. For if they fall, one will lift up his companion. But woe to him who is alone when he falls, for he has no one to help him up. Again, if two lie down together, they will keep warm; but how can one be warm alone? Though one may be overpowered by another, two can withstand him. And a threefold cord is not easily broken. Ecc. 4:9-12

Pastor and author Clarence Macartney wonderfully illustrates the tremendous value and influence that loving friends can have from the life of Ulysses S. Grant. Macartney writes,

General Grant's chief of staff, the Galena lawyer John A. Rawlins, was closer to Grant than any other during the war. It was to Rawlins that Grant gave his pledge that he would abstain from intoxicating liquors. When he broke that pledge Rawlins went to him and with great earnestness pleaded with him, for the sake of himself and for the sake of the great holy cause of the nation, to refrain from strong drink. Faithful were the wounds of a friend. In front of the Capitol at Washington today there stands the magnificent monument of General Grant, sitting on his horse in characteristic pose and flanked on either side by stirring battle scenes. But at the other end of Pennyslvania Avenue, a little to the south of the avenue, is Rawlins Park, where there stands a very commonplace statue of Rawlins. Whenever I stand before the great monument of Grant on his horse there in front of the Capitol, I think of that other monument. I think of that faithful friend who kept Grant on his horse.

We all need people in our lives who can help keep us on our horse. May God grant that we have at least a few. And that we are that kind of friend to others as well.

FLASHPOINT
Vital spirituality is always lived arm in arm.

The Foundation for Community

"And may the Lord make you increase and abound in love to one another…" I Thess.3:12

Community occurs best among overwhelmed saints. Where believers are overwhelmed by the greatness and love of God, staggered by the reality of being indwelt by the three Persons of the Godhead, and reeling under the weight of God's invigorating glory, they move forward toward one another in radically different and better ways. As Paul puts it in this passage, *outflow is predicated upon inflow.* Before we can abound in love to one another, the Lord must first increase (lit. "fill up") His love in us. Eugene Peterson beautifully captures the original Greek of this passage in his paraphrase, *"And may the Master pour on the love so it fills your lives and splashes over on everyone around you."* *(The Message)*

There is a Jewish fable that beautifully describes this. It is the story of two brothers, both farmers, who lived next to one another. After one particularly bountiful harvest, each brother began to decide what he might do with his surplus. The first brother said to himself, "Here I am with a wife and children but my poor brother has no one. I think I'll surprise him by taking some of my crop and placing it in his field."

The other brother thought, "Here I am single. My poor brother has a wife and children to care for and I don't need anywhere near what I have. I think I'll surprise him and put some of my crop in his field." The parable records that the two brothers caught one another at midnight, stealing into the other's field to leave their blessing.

What a beautiful portrait of New Covenant community! I once heard it described it as *"fence-jumping love."* It is moving forward into one another's fields for the purpose of giving from the supernatural bounty provided through glad intimacy with the Father and overwhelming supply of the Spirit. But when the bounty is not there, when we have forfeited our time alone with God, when our hearts are empty, then we approach fellow believers from a very different angle. We look to them to make up for what is missing and become frustrated, discouraged, and even resentful that they are not jumping more quickly into our field to supply our needs.

True fellowship is always grounded foremost in the abundance of God in our fields. Then it is the kind of dynamic fellowship that not only blesses the saints but also powerfully attracts the attention of a love-starved world. Above all else, it is the kind of community which only the triune God makes possible.

> **FLASHPOINT**
> Significant outflow towards others is predicated upon significant inflow from God.

Gifted Community

"Then I will give them one heart and one way..." Jer.32:39

True community is ultimately a supernatural reality. *"I will give..."* is our only hope for the kind of fellowship that most radiantly glorifies God and most deeply satisfies us. Yet, because of this, God-empowered community is also exceedingly elusive. Primarily, I think, because we so easily substitute other things for the touch of God. Yet community—true Christian community—is a supernatural reality or it is nothing. We find it described in Scripture:

"Then I will give them one heart and one way..." (Jer.32:39). *"Then I will give them one heart..."* (Ez.11:19). *"Endeavoring to keep the unity of the Spirit in the bond of peace."* (Eph.4:3) The unity that is *"of the Spirit"* needs only to be maintained, not achieved. This is why the German Lutheran theologian Dietrich Bonhoeffer writes,

> *Christian brotherhood is not an ideal which we must realize; it is rather a reality created by God in Christ in which we may participate. The more clearly we learn to realize that the ground and strength and promise of all our fellowship is in Jesus Christ alone, the more serenely shall we think of our fellowship and pray and hope for it.*

How easily we seek to find unity through means other than Christ! All too often our fellowship is centered on things or activities, rather than God:

- *The church or campus group we belong to*
- *The Christian cause we are most passionate about*
- *The denominational or theological camp we belong to*
- *The kind of schooling for our children*
- *The spiritual experiences we have in common*
- *The political party we are affiliated with*
- *The kind of ministry we are involved in*
- *The Christian leader we most admire*

Genuine Christian community is a unity based on none of the above; but upon a common Christ, Who is the Foundation of a common fellowship, made possible by a common death, indwelt by a common Spirit, and designed for a common purpose. It is God-birthed, Christ-purchased, and Spirit-sustained. It is the kind of community where God is *required* or it will soon fall apart. And it's the only kind of community worth flaunting before a watching world.

> **FLASHPOINT**
> True community is centered around and
> dependent upon Christ.

Present Power of the Resurrection

"But if the Spirit of Him Who raised Christ from the dead dwells in you, He Who raised Christ from the dead will also give life to your mortal bodies through His Spirit who dwells in you." Rom.8:11

This great provision of the New Covenant—*"the Spirit of Him Who raised Christ from the dead"*—forever silences our pleas for exemption from radical godliness. Resurrection power is always greater than the dysfunctionality of our past, the wounds of abuse or neglect, the power of sin, the pressure of outward circumstances, or the phobias of our personal inadequacies. Augustine wrote in his diary once after sinning, *"You fool, do you not know that you carry around God in your body!"*

That is exactly what we are as believers—flesh and blood transporters of God, New Testament tabernacles on the move. Living, breathing tabernacles who are permanently indwelt by *"the Spirit of Him Who raised Christ from the dead,"* as Paul puts it. And indwelling resurrection power trumps every obstacle put before it, if we'll let it.

Contrary to what is often suggested today, there are no saints with so much baggage from their past that they are beyond hope for substantial change in the present. God will handle any amount or kinds of baggage if He is given the opportunity. Certainly, we can choose to block His working. But what we cannot block is the actual, abiding reality of permanent, indwelling, resurrection power lurking within each of us. And many, many times the most important thing we can do is take our eyes off ourselves long enough to remember that there is more to our story than just our flesh. Let me say it again. There is more to our story than just our flesh. Blessedly more.

Thou art a sea without a shore,
Awesome, immense Thou art;
A sea which can contract itself
Within my very heart.
F.W. Faber

> **FLASHPOINT**
> Resurrection power is God's only solution
> to our flesh.

Soft Hearts

"Finally, all of you, live in harmony with one another; be sympathetic, love as brothers, be compassionate and humble." I Peter 3:8

Sympathy. It comes from the combination of two Greek words literally meaning *"to suffer with."* And that really is the ground floor as to how this critical commodity is developed in our lives. Sympathy is best learned in the classroom of actual suffering where one's heart is actually broken and actual tears stream down actual eyes. Where real pain takes up real residence in real lives and leaves real scars as ongoing reminders of its real visitation.

But those scars can leave us different people than we were before. Wonderfully different. If we can manage to not let bitterness set in, we become less judgmental. Less cocky. Less hardened to others' plights. More compassionate. More understanding. More humble. I love the way Adelaide Anne Procter puts it in her poem, "Judge Not:"

Judge not the workings of his brain,
And of his heart thou cannot see.
What looks to thy dim eyes a stain,
In God's pure light may only be
A scar brought from some well-won field
Where thou wouldst only faint and yield.

I love her line, *"A scar brought from some well-won field/Where thou wouldst only faint and yield."* Nothing knocks the stuffing out of arrogance and judgmentalism quite like pain. Pain of being unfairly accused. Pain of watching loved ones suffer. Pain of regret over personal sin and failure. Pain of seemingly unrewarded faithfulness. Pain of betrayal by those closest. On and on it goes. Real pain leaves us with real scars. But those real scars serve to rein in our critical spirit toward others probably more than any other means.

Scarred saints see others' stains differently than most. They are so keenly aware that *"what looks to thy dim eyes a stain"* may very well be a battle *"scar brought from some well-won field/Where thou wouldst only faint and yield."* Pain not only brings scars. If allowed, it also brings what we need most—brokenness. And as well, sympathy. Something that the world needs to see far more of from those of us calling ourselves Christ-followers.

> **FLASHPOINT**
> Our scars enable us to view others' stains far more compassionately.

Playing to the Crowd

"For before certain men came from James, he would eat with the Gentiles; but when they came, he withdrew and separated himself, fearing those who were of the circumcision" Gal.2:12

An old fable has been passed down for generations that tells of an elderly man who was traveling with a boy and a donkey. As they walked through a village, the man was leading the donkey and the boy was walking behind. The townspeople said the old man was a fool for not riding, so to please them he climbed up on the animal's back. When they came to the next village, the people said the old man was cruel to let the child walk while he enjoyed the ride.

So, to please them, he got off and set the boy on the donkey's back and continued on his way. In the third village, people accused the child of being lazy for making the old man walk, and the suggestion was made that they both ride. So to please the villagers, the man climbed on and they set off again, both riding the donkey. In the fourth village, the townspeople were indignant at the cruelty to the donkey because he was made to carry two people. The frustrated man was last seen walking with the boy, both of them helping to carry the donkey as they went down the road!

What a great way to describe the danger of playing to the crowd! It is an absolute no-win proposition. Certainly it is only human to *desire* others' approval, especially those we love and respect the most. But to become *controlled* by their approval is to play the part of the old man in the fable. We all have too many different pairs of eyes looking in on our life to keep everyone's approval intact. At the end of the day, the pair of eyes that monumentally matter the most are the ones looking down from heaven. It is only the deep satisfaction of going for broke in a God-enabled, God-directed assault upon life that can keep us off the bed of thorns of needing others' approval. Or going through life as a donkey carrier.

Take Peter for instance. I love Peter. He provides me with more hope than any other apostle. I'm glad to know that he struggled with something I battle each day—playing to the crowd. Before the men came from James, Peter was enjoying his freedom in Christ and loving the Gentile believers well—*"he would eat with the Gentiles."* When these Jewish believers came everything changed. He *"withdrew and separated himself."* What brought about Peter's change of heart? He was *"fearing those who were of the circumcision."* His commitment to maintain his spiritual status in the eyes of his peers overruled his new freedom that was propelling him into a love-based ministry to the Gentiles.

How easily this can happen to us. I'm struck in this passage by the phrase *"certain men."* There were many men who could not rob Peter of his freedom, but there were *"certain men"* who could. Who are the *"certain men"* in our lives? They are those individuals for whom we will sacrifice our spiritual integrity and spontaneity in order to keep their approval intact. We all have them. Our boss, our spouse, our friends, perhaps even our pastor. *"The fear of man brings a snare, but whoever trusts in the Lord shall be made safe* (lit. 'set on high')." (Pr.29:25) When any human being can keep us chained to their approval, we have lost our freedom in Christ. Paul Tournier, the famed Swiss psychologist writes,

> ...*in all fields, even those of culture and art, other people's judgment exercises a paralyzing effect. Fear of criticism kills spontaneity; it prevents men from showing themselves and expressing themselves freely, as they are. Much courage is needed to paint a picture, to write a book, to erect a building designed along new architectural lines, or to formulate an independent opinion or an original idea.*

The good news is that Peter responded to Paul's rebuke and regained his freedom. The *"certain men"* didn't win the day. And they need not win in our lives.

> **FLASHPOINT**
> Only one pair of eyes is worth playing to—the
> pair that wept over Jerusalem and are quick to
> note every minute, faltering step of faithfulness.

The Fires of Sympathy

"You have caused men to ride over our heads; we went through fire and through water; but You brought us out to a wealthier place." Ps. 66:12

Sympathy does not come easily. Or cheaply. It is purchased on the anvil of life where sovereign blows help perfect and soften at the same time. Part of the *"wealthier place"* we are brought out to is that of a new compassion for fellow anvil occupants. As C.S. Lewis put it in giving some advice to an American friend, *"Think of me as a fellow patient in the same hospital who, having been admitted a little earlier, could give some advice."* Fact is, we are all patients in the hospital life. And those of us who have *"been admitted a little earlier"* are not inclined to condemn our fellow patients for being in the hospital. Rather we can give them advice as a fel-

FIREWOOD—FIRE'S COMMUNITY

low-struggler whose wisdom has been purchased from the school of pain and heartache. Charles Spurgeon, known as "The Prince of Preachers," said so well:

> *There is no learning sympathy except by suffering. It cannot be studied in a book, it must be written on the heart. You must go through the fire if you would have sympathy with others who tread the glowing coals. You must yourself bear the cross if you would feel for those whose life is a burden to them.*

Every blow on the anvil uniquely links us with those who have felt the same blows. *"Blessed be the God and Father of our Lord Jesus Christ, the Father of mercies and God of all comfort, who comforts us in all our tribulation, that we may be able to comfort those who are in any trouble, with the comfort with which we ourselves are comforted by God." (*II Cor. 1:3,4) We have the opportunity to uniquely minister to those who have the same struggles as the ones God has taken us through. A physically disabled saint knows a bond with other disabled saints which none but the disabled can enter into. Parents of a wayward child share a special, instant camaraderie with other parents experiencing the same heartache. Those who have lost a child at birth are able to connect with other bereaved parents in ways that those who have never gone through that fire simply cannot.

God does not waste any blows. Every blow on the anvil comes from a hammer which is held by nail-pierced hands. Every blow must pass divine inspection as to whether it is absolutely necessary. And one day there will be special reward for every nanosecond spent on the anvil. But for today, *the blows help produce bonds.* Bonds of sympathy that can be forged in no other way. Bonds that provide opportunity for entrance into others' lives as nothing else can. Bonds that enable us to become wounded warriors following our great Wounded Warrior into His ongoing ministry of transforming sympathy. What a calling…what a Savior!

> **FLASHPOINT**
> Every blow on the anvil produces a bond for ministry.

Forgiveness

"Then his master, after he had called him, said to him, 'You wicked servant! I forgave you all that debt because you begged me. Should you not also have had compassion on your fellow servant, just as I had pity on you?' And his master was angry, and delivered him to the torturers until he should pay all that was due to him." Matt.18:32-34

The root of unforgiveness is not pain; it is arrogance. This is why we need the parable of Matt. 18:21-35 so badly.

It reminds us that while holding a grudge feels eminently reasonable, it is always disastrous to our spiritual health. Quite simply, unforgiveness is one of the clearest signs that we have abandoned our true role in the universe and have now sought to dramatically elevate our station before God and our fellow man. It is forgetting that we are no more than a *"fellow servant"* with the one whose neck we have our fingers around (Matt. 18:28). It is believing that playing the role of judge and handing down sentence (Matt. 18:30) is something not that far out of our league. Most of all, it is living life with complete amnesia concerning our own need for forgiveness. And the massive amount of forgiveness that the massive amount of our sin requires.

Forgiveness is costly, but refusing to forgive is even more costly. I don't know anyone who has put it better than Frederick Buechner:

> *Of the Seven Deadly Sins, anger is possibly the most fun. To lick your wounds, to smack your lips over grievances long past, to roll over your tongue the prospect of bitter confrontations still to come, to savor to the last toothsome morsel both the pain you are given and the pain you are giving back—in many ways it is a feast fit for a king. The chief drawback is that what you are wolfing down is yourself. The skeleton at the feast is you.*

Exactly right! The *"skeleton at the feast"* is us. Or, as Christ puts it, we are handed over *"to the torturers"* (Matt. 18:34). Torturers such as bitterness, resentment, smoldering anger, sleeplessness, etc.. I say it again—forgiveness is costly but refusing to forgive brings an even higher price tag. We cannot afford not to forgive.

Perhaps then the root of true forgiveness is the opposite of arrogance—genuine brokenness. That humility is the price tag we all pay when we send someone's debt away, which is the essence of forgiveness. I believe this is exactly the case. Yes, it is costly to forgive. It will always cost our ego; it will always bankrupt our pride. There's no such thing as costless forgiveness. But as Reformed theologian Lewis Smedes puts it so well, *"To forgive is to set a prisoner free and discover that the prisoner was you."* We can have *ego* or we can have *freedom*, but we can't have both.

> **FLASHPOINT**
> Holding a grudge charges interest on the
> soul that we can not afford.

Fuel

FIRE'S RESOURCING

"While I was staying at Nailsworth, it pleased the Lord to teach me a truth...the benefit of which I have not lost, though now, while preparing the eighth edition for the press, more than forty years have passed away. The point is this: I saw more clearly than ever, that the first great and primary business to which I ought attend every day was, to have my soul happy in the Lord. The first thing to be concerned about was not, how much I might serve the Lord, how I might glorify the Lord; but how I might get my soul in a happy state, and how my inner man may be nourished."

– GEORGE MUELLER –

F or fire to continue burning, it must be resourced. In other words, it must have fuel and the right kind of fuel. Prairie fires, for instance, are best put out by reducing the available grass and brush through what is called a backfire. I once read in a piece by Nebraska historian Addison Erwin Sheldon that the only way to protect against a high headfire is to start a backfire some distance ahead of it which would burn away the grass and leave nothing to feed it.

When fire has no fuel, it has "nothing to feed it." And when that happens, the flames will soon diminish and the fire will fade. And it is exactly the same in the faith journey! Without proper resourcing our hearts grow cold, our spirits lag, and our vitality evaporates. Though the fire never goes completely out in any believer's heart, without resourcing we can quickly become but a shell of what we were meant to be.

But as we again avail ourselves to the great resources of God; we find the fire within rekindled. The following meditations focus on a few of these more important resources: time alone worshipping and enjoying God, personal brokenness, our identity in Christ, the Holy Spirit within us, and the amazing power of grace.

Our "Christian Duty"

"Ho! Everyone who thirsts, come to the waters; and you who have no money, come, buy and eat. Yes, come, buy wine and milk without money and without price. Why do you spend money for what is not bread, and your wages for what does not satisfy? Listen carefully to Me, and eat what is good, and let your soul delight itself in abundance." Is. 55:1-2

"It is a Christian duty, as you know, for everyone to be as happy as he can." wrote C.S. Lewis. What he meant by this is that God's calling upon our lives is not primarily one of self-denial but of God-devouring. We give up the fool's gold so there is enough room in our hands to seize the true gold—Jesus Himself.

Note the order of the verbs in vs.2—*"listen...eat...delight."* Not *"listen...obey...proclaim"* as many believers would have it. It's as if God is saying, "Take time to fully savor me. Don't just listen, but eat. Don't rush the meal...delight in it." Hmm, maybe *duty* and *delight* are not an oxymoron after all. Perhaps they were always meant to be best of friends.

In the Caribbean I am told that they catch monkeys by drilling a hole through a coconut and placing peanuts inside. The hole is just large enough for the monkey to get his hand through, but too small to get it out unless he lets go of the peanuts. The coconut is then tied to a tree and left out for the unsuspecting monkey. The monkey comes along and slips his hand into the coconut to take hold of the peanuts. Because the monkey is so determined to hold on to the peanuts, he ultimately forfeits his freedom to keep his catch intact. If only he realized the preciousness of what he was giving up by holding on to the peanuts!

Do we not so often do the very same thing? We hold tenaciously to the peanuts of this world—sex, alcohol, ambition, hobbies, cars, work, approval of others, money, religious respectability, etc. because sin has duped us into believing that life can be found in earthly trinkets that provide everything but God. The philospher Blaise Pascal wrote,

> *There once was in man a true happiness of which now remain to him only the mark and empty trace, which he in vain tries to fill from all his surroundings, seeking from things absent the help he does not obtain in things present. But these are all inadequate, because the infinite abyss can only be filled by an infinite and immutable object, that is to say, only by God Himself.*

As Isaiah puts it, we *"spend money for that which is not bread"* and our *"wages for what does not satisfy."* The unalterable reality though is that the quality of life we yearn for and were made for can only be found in a life of shameless gluttony, one of unrestrained feasting upon the Bread of Life. There is no greater freedom or exhilaration than this. But as long as we allow ourselves to settle for the peanuts of earth, this Bread of Heaven will never have the opportunity to delightfully satisfy our divinely implanted taste-buds. God calls us to give up the peanuts so there is enough room in our mouths for the best, namely Him and

His unrivaled presence. And this my friend, is a "Christian duty" we can all live with. No—live by.

> **FLASHPOINT**
> The preeminent reason to give up the trinkets is to make room for the Treasure.

Dragged Away

"And she had a sister called Mary, who also sat at Jesus' feet and heard His word. But Martha was distracted with much serving..." Lk. 10:39-40

Ouch. How often I have read this passage, and yet too often find myself still following in Martha's footsteps. I so long to be more like Mary, refusing to let anything get in the way of knowing Christ more deeply and passionately than ever. But things do get in the way. Some bad, like lust and greed and ego. Some good, like meetings and speaking and serving. Just like Martha.

This passage is especially colorful in the original Greek. The word for *"distracted"* means *"to be pulled or dragged away."*

What an interesting way of putting it! Martha allowed herself to be dragged away from what she needed most—time alone at the feet of Jesus. But what was it that dragged her away? The word for *"serving"* is the exact Greek word which is very often translated *"ministry."* Thus we could just as easily translate this passage, *"But Martha was dragged away by much ministry."* Is anybody reading this able to relate besides me? I'm guessing so.

Henry Martyn was greatly used by the Lord as a missionary and bible translator in the early 1800's. He unwittingly wrote of the secret of his fruitfulness in his journal, *"My principal enjoyment is the enjoyment of His presence."* Ah, what a great description of living as a Mary. But in the same journal he also wrote of the times he became more like Martha—*"The want of private devotional reading and shortness of prayers through incessant sermon making has produced much strangeness between God and my soul."* I deeply appreciate his honesty; it provides hope for all of us.

Years ago I heard the renowned Latin evangelist Luis Palau ask his audience, "What's the first thing a Christian should do with his salvation?" Now the answer to that question was utterly predictable. Whenever an evangelist/missionary asks a question like that, you know what's coming. Any evangelist worth his salt, any missionary back on furlough, will tell you the same thing—"give it away, share it with others, proclaim it to your friends..." or something to that effect. And when one of the world's foremost evangelist/missionaries poses the question...well, we all know what's on its way.

That's why Luis's answer caught me completely off guard. Delightfully so. And that's probably why I remember it to this day. He looked out over the audience and with that great smile of his said emphatically, "Enjoy it! The very first thing every Christian should do with their salvation is to take time to enjoy it to the hilt." In other words, be a Mary.

Ministry is a good thing. But time alone with Christ is a *better* thing. An infinitely better thing. Fight for it. Refuse to surrender it. Let nothing drag you away from those solitary times alone at Christ's feet, gazing into the face of Him Who is "altogether lovely," and hanging onto every word that cascades from His mouth. Let other things go, but not Him. Choose the good part which will never be taken from you (Lk. 10:42). It not only restores our soul and reignites our passion. In the final analysis, it is also determines whether His touch hangs heavy upon our ministry or not.

> **FLASHPOINT**
> *Knowing* Christ is more important than *serving* Him.

Near Enough?

"Oh, send out Your light and Your truth! Let them lead me; let them bring me to Your holy hill and to Your tabernacle. Then I will go to the altar of God, to God my exceeding joy; and on the harp I will praise You, O God, my God." Ps. 43:3-4

Did you notice the progression *"to Your holy hill...to Your tabernacle...to the altar of God...to God"*? There is a great danger for all of us in drawing near to God. It is that we draw near, but just not near enough. It is the peril of stopping just short of the absolute best He has to offer us Himself. Of settling for close proximity rather than ravishing oneness.

Some saints are satisfied with simply making it to His *"holy hill."* Others press on to His *"tabernacle."* Still others make it all the way *"to the altar of God."* But the highest prize and deepest joy is reserved only for those who personally and passionately take hold of *"God"* for themselves. He alone qualifies as *"my exceeding joy."* Going to church is good, but it is not enough. Listening to a great sermon is good, but it is not enough. Being part of an awesome worship service is good, but it is not enough. Warm fellowship with like-minded believers is good, but it is not enough. Our deepest needs can only, but only, be met through vitally encountering God Himself. Augustine wrote of this extensively in his "Confessions":

Oh! That I might repose on Thee! Oh! That Thou wouldest enter my heart, and inebriate it, that I may forget my ills, and embrace Thee, my sole good!

How sweet all at once it was for me to be rid of those fruitless joys which I had once feared to lose! You drove them from me, you who are the true, the sovereign joy. You drove them from me and took their place, you who are sweeter than all pleasure.

But one of my favorite quotes on this comes from J. Oswald Sanders,

Christ is claiming the ability to satisfy the deepest need of the human heart, yet we are strangely reluctant to come directly to Him. We will attend ceremonies and observe sacraments. We will follow men and congregate in meetings. We will frequent camps and conventions. We will listen to priests and preachers—anything, it would seem, except come personally and alone into the presence of Christ. But He is absolutely intolerant. He will quench our spiritual thirst personally and not by proxy.

I love his thought, *"But He is absolutely intolerant. He will quench our spiritual thirst personally and not by proxy."* Amen! May God grant us the wisdom to know where and when we are trying to quench our thirst through proxy. And the courage and determination to draw near enough for Him to satisfy us personally. Nothing else will do the job.

> **FLASHPOINT**
> Refuse to settle for anything less than God's
> best. Namely, Himself.

Roots

"The root of the righteous yields fruit." Pr.12:12

"...Their root is dried up; They shall bear no fruit." Hos.9:16

One would think it should read, *"The branch of the righteous yields fruit."* But the fact is that roots are of far greater importance in fruit-bearing than branches. They're just not as visible. Yet for the tree, nothing matters more than its roots. Stability, vitality, and fruitfulness are ultimately determined deep beneath the ground, at root level. And so it is with God's children. Contentment of soul and significance of life are determined by the health of our roots more than by anything else. Period.

A.W. Tozer has written a wonderful book entitled "The Root of the Righteous." In it he notes,

The bough that breaks off from the tree in a storm may bloom briefly and give to the unthinking passer-by the impression that it is a healthy and fruitful branch, but its tender blossoms will soon perish and the bough itself wither and die. There is no lasting life apart from the root. Much that passes for Christianity today is the brief bright effort of the severed branch to bring forth its fruit in its season.

I love his statement, *"There is no lasting life apart from the root."*

George Muller was an incredibly fruitful servant of God. During his lifetime he helped build five large orphanages housing some ten thousand orphans, of whom approximately one-third came to know Christ. He received and gave away some seven and a half million dollars to support hundreds of missionaries. He was heavily involved in Christian publishing and the founding of many educational and religious institutions. From age seventy to eighty-four he traveled more than two hundred thousand miles in forty-two different countries, preaching the gospel to more than three million people.

His secret? Roots. Deep, robust, God-thirsty roots. In his journal he writes,

While I was staying at Nailsworth, it pleased the Lord to teach me a truth...the benefit of which I have not lost, though now, while preparing the eighth edition for the press, more than forty years have passed away. The point is this: I saw more clearly than ever, that the first great and primary business to which I ought attend every day was, to have my soul happy in the Lord. The first thing to be concerned about was not, how much I might serve the Lord, how I might glorify the Lord; but how I might get my soul in a happy state, and how my inner man may be nourished.

I love the way he puts it—*"...the first great and primary business to which I ought attend every day was, to have my soul happy in the Lord."* The fragrant, fruitful life of George Muller is a powerful and lasting testimony to the surpassing importance of giving preeminent attention to our roots. Not just rote bible study or mechanical praying, but deep, passionate, white-hot God-seeking. This and this alone produces men and women whose souls are *"happy in the Lord."* May we be counted among them.

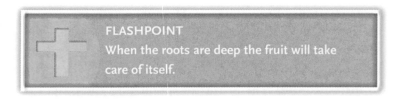

FLASHPOINT
When the roots are deep the fruit will take care of itself.

Qualified for Ministry

"Come now, therefore, and I will send you to Pharaoh that you may bring My people, the children of Israel, out of

Egypt. But Moses said to God, 'Who am I that I should go to Pharaoh, and that I should bring the children of Israel out of Egypt?' So He said, 'I will certainly be with you...'" Ex.3:10-12

There is a difference between being *equipped* for ministry and *qualified* for ministry. A huge difference. Let me illustrate. If there were a professional football team that would allow it, I could go into the locker room before the game, put on all the football gear and uniform, and then walk out onto the field with the team. I would be equipped to play the game, but would I be qualified to play? You don't have to laugh that hard! Obviously not.

Seminary or Bible college training, bible studies, discipleship groups, mentoring, etc. are all very helpful for equipping saints for ministry. But none of these things qualify for ministry. What then qualifies? I believe we find a large part of the answer in God's calling of Moses.

Moses is eighty years old when God meets up with him on the backside of the Midian desert. His first forty years were spent being marvelously equipped to lead God's people. Acts 7:22 describes his preparedness: *"And Moses was learned in all the wisdom of the Egyptians, and was mighty in words and deeds."* Josephus records a great victory which Moses orchestrated on behalf of the Egyptians against the Ethiopians—*"When [Moses] had therefore proceeded thus on his journey, he came upon the Ethiopians before they expected him; and, joining battle with them, he beat them, and deprived them of the hopes they had of success against the Egyptians, and went on in overthrowing their cities, and indeed made a great slaughter of these*

Ethiopians." (Josephus' Writings Book 2, Chapter.10)

But when Moses went out to serve God at age forty he literally butchered the job. In his own strength, in his own timing, and in his own wisdom, he murdered an Egyptian and had to flee the country (Ex. 2:11-15) For the next forty years he tended sheep for his father-in-law in Midian (Ex.3:1) But finally he was becoming *qualified* for ministry. When God calls him to the mighty task of delivering His people from Egypt, Moses has but one response. *"Who am I that I should go...and that I should deliver..."* (Ex.3:11) And this response demonstrates that he is finally qualified to be used of God in a significant way. He is a deeply broken man, utterly despairing of any natural ability to pull off what God has called him to. He is a remarkably different man than forty years before. And that difference is what puts him in the position of being used by God and not merely working for God. And note—please note—God doesn't try to talk him out of his inadequacy. He simply states, *"I will certainly be with you."* This is God's only solution to our permanent, unrelieved inadequacy. But it's the only solution we need.

What most qualifies us for ministry is not a certificate of ordination but a certificate of desperation. The unwavering, steadfast belief that in our own native abilities we don't have what it takes and never will. That Christ's words *"apart from Me you can do nothing"* (Jn. 15:4-5) are not hyperbole but wholly unexaggerated truth. I have heard it put, *"God will never call you to something you can do. He will only call you to that which requires Him."* Moses would have echoed a hearty amen to that statement at age eighty. But not at forty. And that's why he was equipped but not qualified.

The other thing that qualifies us for ministry is *availability* (Ex.4:12-14). When *brokenness* and *availability* go hand in hand, it is an awesome thing to see what God can do through a person's life. Your life. My life. Any life that has come to the very end of its rope, despairs of ever having what it takes and then throws itself back in desperate dependency upon the God of the burning bush. And then hangs on for the ride. And what a ride it will be! Just ask Moses.

FLASHPOINT
The end of ourselves is the beginning of God.

New Identity

"For you died, and your life is hidden with Christ in God. When Christ who is our life appears, then you also will appear with Him in glory." Col. 3:3-4

Christ is not simply a ticket to heaven or a great addition to our lives. He *"is our life"* as Paul puts it, and our personal identity is now swallowed up in Him. What frees us from the paralyzing grip of inferiority and inadequacy is not the power of positive thinking, but the astonishing wonder of united identity. God never sees us without seeing Christ first. We do well to follow His lead. As believers we no longer have the option of thinking about ourselves apart from the indwelling Christ to Whom we are inseparably united. Our life *"is hidden with Christ in God"* and it will never be found outside of Him. At least in God's sight, which is ultimately the only sight that really matters. Read what Martin Luther and John Calvin have said about this breathtaking reality:

> *...thou art so entirely joined unto Christ, that He and thou art made as it were one person: so that thou mayest boldly say, I am now one with Christ, that is to say, Christ's righteousness, victory, and life are mine. And again, Christ may say, I am that sinner, that is, his sins and his death are Mine, because he is united and joined unto Me, and I unto him.* Martin Luther

> *Before my conversion, had you knocked at the door of my heart and asked who lives there, I would have said, 'Martin Luther lives here.' Had you come in to see me, you would have found a monk with his head shaved, sleeping in a hair shirt, under his head two tables of stone, a scourge hanging down by the side of the bed. But now if you knock at the door of my heart and ask who lives there, I will reply: 'Martin Luther no longer lives here; Jesus the Lord lives here now.'* Martin Luther

The moment I consider Christ and myself as two, I am gone.
Martin Luther

We ought not to separate Christ from ourselves or ourselves from Him. John Calvin

A healthy, godly self-image is never *developed*, but just simply *received*. The focal point of our personal identity is the inexhaustible sufficiency and overwhelming beauty of the Savior to Whom we are now perfectly and unalterably fused together with. What we have is not so much self-esteem as Christ-esteem. And this allows us to have a joyful, humble, and relaxed self-image, one that isn't grasping for proof of personal adequacy.

Our internal sense of worth is God-given, God-sustained, God-absorbed, and God-glorifying. The data for our core belief concerning who we are and what we are worth is supernaturally and unalterably inscribed within. Our search for significance is at last over, because of Christ's ever-present, ever-powerful Personhood within us. And because of this, we are at last freed from the need to prove ourselves in this world. And that my friend, is truly a blessed relief!

> **FLASHPOINT**
> God never sees us without seeing Christ first.
> Follow His lead!

Charmed Towards Righteousness

"...the goodness of God is meant to lead you to repentance."
Rom. 2:4

People are most powerfully transformed not by predict-able threats, but by surprising kindness. The bible calls it "grace." Grace is God's passionate, irrational, incompre-hensible kindness. It is a word that is so often used among believers that we have become calloused to its intended impact in our lives. Yet it is the heart and soul of our lives as New Testament saints.

Nothing arrests and transforms the soul of man like the power of true grace. David Brainerd, the early American missionary to the Indians, discovered the great reality of this in his ministry among them:

> *I never got away from Jesus and Him crucified. When my people were gripped by this great evangelical doctrine of Christ and Him crucified, I had no need to give them instructions about morality...I find that my Indians begin to put on the garments of holiness and their common life begins to be sanctified even in small matters when they are possessed by the doctrine of Christ and Him crucified.*

What an intriguing observation—*"I had no need to give them instructions about morality."* While it is true that grace can be abused (Rom.6:1), let us also never forget that it turns people's lives inside out for the glory of God like nothing else. It is God's goodness rather than His judgment that tends to bring about the deepest change of heart in a person's life. When one is caught off guard by the lavish display of a goodness not deserved, when the slow moving prodigal is run over by the Father's passionate love, when hardness of heart is met with nail-pierced hands, something inside of us begins to melt. And that melting is often the beginning of deep repentance. Theologian Reinhold Niebuhr put it so well,

> *You may be able to compel people to maintain certain minimum standards by stressing duty, but the highest moral and spiritual achievements depend not upon a push but a pull. People must be charmed into righteousness.*

"People must be charmed into righteousness." What a marvelous way to express the power of surprising, radically unexpected grace. How then does God get this grace from heaven to earth? Through the person of Christ, first and foremost. But there are other ways as well. High among them is clothing grace in living flesh. In other words, you...me...us. Men and women who, like Paul, have been arrested by pursuant, scandalous kindness on our own Damascus road—and then turn around to be the pursuers. One of our highest callings on this dark planet is to be living, breathing, surprise visitations of God's passionate, irrational love. What a calling! What a privilege! And what a blessed escape from rote, drab, duty-driven spirituality.

> **FLASHPOINT**
> Grace reaches places in the human heart
> which justice never can.

Torrents of Blessing

"On the last day, that great day of the feast, Jesus stood and cried out saying, 'If anyone thirsts, let him come to Me and drink. He who believes in Me, as the Scripture has said, out of his heart will flow rivers of living water.' But this He spoke concerning the Spirit, whom those believing in Him would receive; for the Holy Spirit was not yet given, because Jesus was not yet glorified." Jn.7:37-39

Child of God, there is far more to you than you may think. Or perhaps better, far more *in* you than you may think. The word translated here *"rivers"* is very frequently translated *"floods"* (Matt.7:25-27; Rev.12:15-16). *"Torrents"* is another possible rendering of the Greek. So what's the point? Very simple. You, my friend, are home to a spiritual deluge, with torrents of divine waters pressing forward for release from deep within. As Oswald Chambers writes, *"If you believe in Jesus, you will find that God has nourished in you mighty torrents of blessings for others."* We have an overflowing river within us called the Holy Spirit, a river that can never be drained or even diminished. Our cup isn't full; it *"runneth over"* (Ps.23:5).

Now I'm very aware that quite often it does not feel like there are torrents of living waters within. Fact is, many times we would be glad just for some trickles! Yet we must be so very, very careful not to dismiss or downplay the extravagance of what God's word holds forth simply because the level of our present experience hasn't scaled the heights of our Lord's offer. The British evangelical Dr. Martyn Lloyd Jones put it so well when he wrote concerning the balance of truth and experience:

There are two main ways in which...we can go wrong in this question of the relationship of our experiences to the teachings of scripture. The first danger is that of claiming things which either go beyond the scriptures or which, indeed, may even be contrary to it...There are many (and they generally are the more spiritually minded) who are always prone to become so interested in the experimental side that they become indifferent to the scriptures...

But there is a second danger and it is equally important that we should keep it in mind. The second danger is the exact opposite of the first, as these things generally go from one violent extreme to the other...The second danger, then, is that of being satisfied with something very much less than what is offered in the Scripture, and the danger of interpreting Scripture by our ex-

*periences and reducing its teaching to the level of what we know
and experience…People come to the New Testament and, instead
of taking its teaching as it is, they interpret it in light of their
experience, and so they reduce it.*

Do you see what he is saying? It is so, so important!
When our experience does not match what the scriptures
appear to offer, we must beware of the subtle danger of
interpreting the passage in such a way that we bring God's
word *down* to the level of our experience—thereby quietly
vindicating our lack of experience. Rather we should pray
that God would *raise* our experience to the level of the passage and save us at all costs from downsizing the magnitude of the offer He delights to see us taking Him up on.

FLASHPOINT
Beware of downsizing God's offer just
because we haven't experienced it yet.

Flames
FIRE'S ESSENCE

*"God has used a number of…similitudes to hint at
His incomprehensible being, and judging from the Scriptures
one would gather that His favorite similitude is fire…
As a fire He spoke to Moses from the burning bush; in the fire
He dwelt above the camp of Israel through all the wilderness
journey; as fire He dwelt between the wings of the cherubim
in the Holy of Holies; to Ezekiel He revealed Himself as a
strange brightness of "a fire infolding itself."*

— A.W. TOZER —

"For our God is a consuming fire."

— HEB.12:29 —

I n the bible, God is likened to many things—*father, master, nursing mother, rock, fountain, etc. But He is likened unto fire over ninety times in scripture. I believe Tozer is exactly right*—"God has used a number of...similitudes to hint at His incomprehensible being, and judging from the Scriptures one would gather that His favorite similitude is fire." *This has to be a paradigm shift of monumental proportions to many, if not most Christians today. There is nothing timid, tame, or safe about God. Mr. Beaver explains it clearly to to Lucy in C.S. Lewis's* The Lion, the Witch and the Wardrobe *when he answers her question about Aslan,* "'Then he isn't safe?' said Lucy. 'Safe?' said Mr. Beaver. 'Don't you hear what Mrs. Beaver tells you? Who said anything about safe? 'Course he isn't safe. But he's good. He's the King, I tell you.'"

The flames of a fire can do many things. They can warm chilled hands. They can provide light in the dark. They can cook our food. But they can also wreak unspeakable devastation with uncontrollable fury, consuming everything in their path. Just like our God. These meditations are devoted to the critical need to approach God as He is, to "behold the goodness and severity of God" *(Rom. 11:22) To help us see afresh the God revealed in the scriptures—the King high and lifted up, Whose wrath burns furiously against sin and Whose mercy burns even more passionately towards sinners.*

More than Love

"Inasmuch as there is none like You, O Lord (You are great, and Your name is great in might), who would not fear You, O King of the nations? For this is Your rightful due....But the Lord is the true God; He is the living God and the everlasting King. At His wrath the earth will tremble, and the nations will not be able to endure his indignation." Jer.10:6-7,10

Certainly God is love. And how desperately fortunate for us that He is. But that is not all God is, nor is it all that He is capable of being. Or obligated to be. Yes, He is a loving Father, an exceedingly gracious Provider, a merciful and forgiving God. Yet He is also the dread Sovereign of the universe. Like it or not, God will judge every man by His perfect and unalterable standard. Man can seek to wish away this certainty, can vainly attempt to recreate God in the mold of his own self-serving interests, or neuter Him by reducing Him only to love. But God remains exactly the kind of God He is, whether He is given the go ahead by man or not. John White writes about this very issue in a powerful chapter of *The Race* entitled "The God of White-Hot Rage."

'The God of White-Hot Rage'—does my title sound extreme? Perhaps. But you see, I'm not interested in the kind of God we want to believe in, but the God who really is. We Christians are idolaters...We may not carve him (God) out of wood, but we do try to forget the uncomfortable parts of him and shape him to our

own personal comfort.

I once read an article by a man who called himself an evangelical yet talked about 'the kind of God I would feel comfortable with.' He, at least was being honest about doing what we all do—making God into a sort of holy Teddy Bear.

Later he writes, *"We are not called to be God's public-relations experts but to be witnesses. The only image we must project is the correct one. We aren't to aim for effect. God's character is not a subject for a media campaign designed to present His best face."*

I love his thought, *"We may not carve [God] out of wood, but we do try to forget the uncomfortable parts of him and shape him to our own personal comfort."* How well put! The natural propensity of modern man is not to carve an idol out of wood. We're too sophisticated for that. Rather we carve out of the true and living God those attributes that make us most uncomfortable. And leave those attributes that make God most manageable. And usable. Theological-ethicist Richard Niebuhr put it well when he described the modern church's presentation of Christianity as *"A God without wrath brought men without sin into a kingdom without judgment through the ministrations of a Christ without a cross."* So true!

Nothing does this better than the creation of a love-only, kindness-only, sweetness-only God. Then we try to promote to the world this manageable, usable God as the One men and women should invite to run their lives. The problem however is that a manageable, usable God is not qualified to run the universe. Or mighty enough to run anyone's life. Or awesome enough to take our breath away. And if the God we worship does not take our breath away, sooner or later we will begin to yawn at Him.

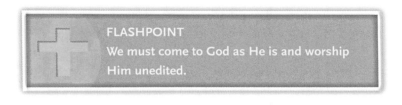

FLASHPOINT
We must come to God as He is and worship Him unedited.

The Lion and the Lamb

"... 'Do not weep, Behold the Lion of the tribe of Judah, the Root of David, has prevailed to open the scroll and loose its seven seals.' And I looked, and behold ...stood a Lamb..."
Rev.5:5-6

The love of God and His offer of forgiveness will never amaze us unless it is seen against the backdrop of God's raging fury towards sin. If one's view of God is that He is exclusively love, then there will be no surprise element whatsoever to that love. His forgiveness and mercy towards us will be wholly assumed since that is His fundamental job description as God. In fact, that is exactly what

H.G.Wells said at the end of his life when someone asked him if he had experienced God's forgiveness. Wells, no friend to Christianity, responded, *"Forgiveness. Of course God forgives, that's His business."*

A.W. Tozer writes, *"The vague and tenuous hope that God is too kind to punish the ungodly has become a deadly opiate for the consciences of millions. It hushes their fears and allows them to practice all pleasant forms of iniquity while death draws every day nearer and the command to repent goes unregarded."*

It's much like Mr. Rogers. When Mr. Rogers is nice to the kids in his neighborhood, is there anything surprising about it? Of course not. Niceness is all he knows how to be. What would be surprising is if he ever kicked a kid! That's what I've been waiting to see.

Assumed grace can never be transforming grace. It simply has no punch to it, no fizz, no sparkle. This is why John's first picture of Christ in Rev.5 was *"the Lion of the tribe of Judah"*(Rev.5:5). After beholding the Lion, he then saw *"a Lamb as though it had been slain"*(Rev.5:6). The order in inviolable. Jesus will never be appreciated as Lamb unless He is first encountered as Lion. God's love will never thrill our souls as long as it is seen as His *obligation* rather than His *gift*.

Imagine with me for a moment that we are at a zoo. As we are looking at the animals, you reach down and pet the head of a small lamb. As you do, the lamb lifts its head and licks your hand. You think, "That's nice," but move on to the other animals. Suddenly someone yells, "Look out!" and you turn around to see what the commotion is about.

But it's too late. Standing right in front of you is the biggest, fiercest lion you have ever seen. He has just escaped its cage and you are his lunch if he so chooses. There is no way to escape. Slowly he moves toward you, opening his jaws wider and wider. Then when he gets right up to you, he reaches out and licks your hand and stands peacefully at your side. You breathe a huge sigh of relief. Let me ask you a question. Which lick would mean more to you, the lick of the lion or that of the lamb? Obviously, the lion. Why? Because the lion could crush you in his jaws just as easily as lick your hand, but the lamb doesn't have that option. The primary reason we are not astonished and exuberant at the Lamb's forgiveness of our sins is that we have too little sense of the Lion's raging fury against our sins. Until we have trembled on death row we will not dance at the granting of our pardon.

> **FLASHPOINT**
> The Lion must precede the Lamb for us to be astonished by grace.

The Need for an Uncomfortable God

"And even now the ax is laid to the root of the trees. There-fore every tree which does not bear good fruit is cut down and thrown into the fire...His winnowing fan is in His hand, and He will thoroughly clean out His threshing floor, and gather His wheat into the barn; but He will burn up the chaff with unquenchable fire." Matt. 3:10-12

Near the end of his life, Henry David Thoreau was asked by his aunt Louisa, *"Have you made your peace with God?"* To this he cynically responded, *"I did not know we had ever quarreled."* Though spoken almost 150 years ago, these words well summarize the condition of modern man—at least it seems to me.

Most people today are wholly comfortable with God. They are utterly at ease with the Maker of the universe and their souls. There is seemingly no dread of one day standing before an infinitely holy God to give account of one's life. As it says in Romans 3:18, *"there is no fear of God before their eyes."* And I believe at least part of the reason for this is that the "hellfire and brimstone" sermon has of-ficially taken its place with the dinosaurs. For all practical purposes, it is extinct.

When was the last time you heard a full out message on the wrath of God and Hell? Not a passing, shy mention of it as part of the message. And certainly not the almost gleeful, fist-pounding ordeal that characterized past generations. But a tearful, compassionate pleading for the unsaved to flee from the fiery, eternal wrath to come? To my shame I haven't given one in a long time...until last Sunday. And it changed me.

As I was preparing for the message, I became absolutely overwhelmed by a simple but critical truth that I had all but lost sight of. The most important thing about Christianity is not what it does for us in this life, but in the life to come. Yes, there are great and wonderful benefits in this life when one trusts Christ alone for the forgiveness of sin. But none of them even remotely compares with the astonishing and exhilarating reality of permanently exchanging that place *"where their worm does not die and the fire is not quenched"* (Mk.9:46) for the new place where *"God will wipe away every tear from their eyes; there shall be no more death, nor sorrow, nor crying. There shall be no more pain, for the former things have passed away."* (Rev.21:4) And in our day of instant gratification, immediate results, here and now living, it is easy to succumb to the spirit of the age and make our gospel presentations almost exclusively present-oriented.

In other words, we invite people to come to Christ for all the things He can provide for us in this life. But, as former Bishop of Canterbury John Tillotson put it so well, *"He who provides for this life, but takes no care for eternity, is wise for a moment, but a fool forever."* People need to know that God *does* have a quarrel with them, and that this quarrel can be settled only at the cross. And that it *must* be settled before they die. From where I sit, the hellfire and brimstone message—properly communicated—is badly in need of resurrection.

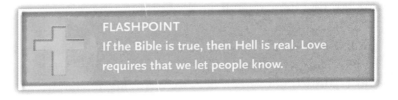

God Most Usable

"Indeed he makes a god and worships it; He makes a carved image and falls down to it. He burns half of it in the fire... and the rest of it he makes into a god...". Is.43:21

Man suffers from a strange malady called *"reverse creationism."* Somehow we have managed to believe that it is okay for us—created human beings—to create a God fashioned to our own liking. That there is nothing wholly insane with the creature begetting the Creator, one that we are wholly comfortable with. One Who is on duty 24/7 in case we need help beyond ourselves. And especially One Whose highest purpose in existence is to meet our needs and further our desires. C.S. Lewis puts it so well concerning the average man's view of God: *"We regard God as an airman regards his parachute; it's there for emergencies but he hopes he'll never have to use it."*

Most of all, this humanly fashioned God is extraordinarily usable. In fact, that seems to be his primary attribute. Beyond that He is disposable. Once utilized to meet our needs, we can quickly toss him aside. Until we need him again, that is.

But America has not cast God off. Far from it. In fact, we have carefully reserved an honored place for Him—in the servants' quarters. After all, who would be foolish enough to do away completely with the best help to be found anywhere? At all costs, we need to keep God around so He can come through for us when everything else has failed. And this is what we label *"calling on God."* I've heard it quipped, *"Most people want to serve God, but only in an advisory capacity."*

The bumper sticker speaks for many with its slogan, *"God is my copilot."* We have supposedly honored God by extending Him a place in the cockpit of our lives, turned to Him in times of emergency, and even invited His input on how we can make our lives fly as smoothly and successfully as possible. Just a casual look around the average Christian bookstore reveals that a sizeable percentage of books are written basically on how to use God. The message they convey is clear and predictable: God is absolutely essential for making life work, and one's approach to finances, politics, health, family, psychology, etc. all must include

Him and His principles in order to succeed. And while there is a modicum of truth in all this, too often Jesus is presented as a kind of divine genie, waiting to grant our wishes and requests if we can just find the right formula for utilizing Him.

Whoever this God is, He is in no way the God of the scriptures. From Genesis to Revelation we find a very unsettling and, at the same time, wonderfully exhilarating truth—God does not exist for us, we exist for Him. *"This people I have formed for Myself..."* (Is. 43:21) is the Magna Charta of our existence.

Eugene Nida, president of the American Bible Society, put it so well, *"The church of North America has become so success oriented that we go from seminar to seminar on how to use God. But few are sitting in quiet holiness asking 'How can God use me?'"* Tragically, he's exactly right. But the great thing about it all is this—we can be part of the few!

FLASHPOINT
God does not exist for us, we exist for Him.

Something to Shout About

"...And your life is hidden with Christ in God." Col.3:3

So here's the question: When God looks down on you, what is His response? Or to put it another way, when our Lord gazes upon you and me, what is the expression on His face? Ever think about that? Is He joyful? Sad? Disappointed? Upset? Or just stoic and expressionless?

The pastor David A. Seamands writes:

> *God's demands of me were so high, and his opinion of me was so low, there was no way for me to live except under his frown...All day long he nagged me: 'Why don't you pray more? Why don't you witness more? When will you ever learn self-discipline?'... God was always using His love against me. He'd show me His nail-pierced hands, and then He would look at me glaringly and say, 'Well, why aren't you a better Christian. Get busy and live the way you ought to'...When I came down to it, there was scarcely a word or a feeling or a thought or a decision of mine that God really liked.*

These words were written before a life-changing encounter with God's grace and a new appreciation for perfect acceptance in Him. And when it happened, it uncovered a truth which I hope none of us ever shakes free from. When God looks down at you, me, and anyone who is in Christ, *He is smiling from ear to ear!* His eyes are dancing with delight while He sings over you and dances around you.

KINDLING FOR THE FIRE

*"The LORD your God in your midst, the Mighty One, will save; He will rejoice over you with gladness, He will quiet you with His love, He will rejoice over you with singing." (*Zeph. 3:17)

But is this really true? And if so, then why? Very simple. God cannot see you before He first sees Jesus. Let me say it again—God cannot see you without first going through Jesus. *"...your life is hidden with Christ in God."* (Col.3:13) *"to the praise of the glory of His grace, by which He made us accepted* (lit. "highly favored") *in the Beloved."* (Eph.1:6)

God cannot look upon His Son without the broadest smile possible creasing His face and explosive joy rising in His heart. *"This is My beloved Son, in Whom I am well pleased,"* He fairly shouted 2,000 years ago when he ripped the heavens wide open to make that proclamation. And those of us in Christ live in the rainforest of God's exuberant and incessant delight in His Son dripping down on us every day. Every hour. Every moment. This does not mean God is not angry, grieved, or saddened at our sinful actions or attitudes. But our *actions* and *attitudes* are dramatically different from our *personhood*. It's the difference between saying, "Your hair is out of place" and "You're ugly." Yes, many times our hair is out of place. But in God's eyes, we are never, ever, ever ugly. We are clothed from head to toe with a gifted, heavenly beauty which infinitely outstrips the best beauty of even angels. Our *"life is hidden with Christ."* Please don't ever recover from that. God is passionately and incessantly moving forward toward you in gladsome love because of your inseparable oneness with His Son. And if that's not something worth shouting about, I'm not sure what is.

> **FLASHPOINT**
> God cannot see you before He sees Jesus.
> Enjoy...then worship...then serve.

Idolatry

"Therefore put to death your members which are upon the earth: fornication, uncleaness...and covetousness, which is idolatry." Col.3:5

Augustine contended that the root of all sin was idolatry. If he is right (and I believe he is), then what exactly is idolatry? This passage in Colossians gives us tremendous help in answering this critical question. According to Paul, covetousness *is* idolatry. What then, is covetousness? The word *"covetousness"* normally conjures up images of greed and avarice. But there is nothing inherent within the word concerning money or possessions. It comes from the combination of two Greek words. One means *"to have or hold"* and the other means *"more."* Literally, it means to *"have or hold more."* More money, more sex, more pleasure, more prestige, ...the list is seemingly endless.

Essentially, idolatry is the heart's defiant response to disappointment or seeming deprivation. It is quietly but fiercely saying to God, "Who you are in and of Yourself (Your Person) and what you have provided for me at this time (Your provisions) are simply not enough. They are not meeting the deep needs of my being and I will...I must... have more!" This is exactly what happened in the garden. Adam and Eve decided they had to have more than the satisfying presence of God and the abundance of the garden. For life to upgrade to all it could be, they had to have more. They had to have fruit from the forbidden tree. And "more" instantly became "less."

Idolatry in all its subtle forms is the requirement for more. More than God Himself. More than what He has presently and legitimately provided. As pastor and authorTim Keller puts it, *"An idol is whatever you look at and say, in your heart of hearts, 'If I have that, then I'll feel my life has meaning, then I'll know I have value, then I'll feel significant and secure.'...If anything in life becomes more fundamental than God to your happiness, meaning in life, and identity, then it is an idol."*

Whether it be sex, money, ambition, or possibly even ministry, Augustine is exactly right. The root of every sin in our lives is ultimately idolatry. It is believing the age old lie of the serpent that God talks a big game but in the pinch He can't or won't come through.

And that is the beauty of our Lord in the wilderness. It was there that He called Satan's bluff and refused the "more" that was dangled before Him. It was there, in the worst of all possible conditions, that His responses screamed to the universe, "God, Who You are in and of Yourself; and what You have provided for me at this point and time... are enough. I have no need for more." If the root of all sin is idolatry, then perhaps the root of all righteousness is God-enamored satisfaction. John Piper writes, *"God is most glorified in us when we are most satisfied in Him."* May God grant that our *more* increasingly be Him and Him alone.

> **FLASHPOINT**
> The genesis of all sin is the deep suspicion that God can't or won't give us what we believe we need most.

Too Comfortable with God

"And the twenty-four elders who sat before God on their thrones fell on their faces and worshiped God," Rev.11:16

Worship is not "hanging out" with God. It is anything but casual, light-hearted chatting with a best buddy. That's not to say that genuine worship isn't characterized by vital communion and the wondrous, mysterious intermingling of God's Spirit with our own. And yes, Christ now calls us *"friends"* (Jn.15:15). But when it is all said and done, worship is still an *on one's face* encounter. At least that's what the twenty four elders in the book of Revelation discovered. And we do well to follow their lead.

If anyone could have claimed a right to casual conversing with the Maker of the universe, it would be them. After all, they had spiritually qualified to sit on thrones before God. But their worship was anything but casual or comfortable. Like all of us, they were still created beings in the presence of unspeakably majestic, uncreated Perfection. And their approach to worship was stunned awe and prostrate reverence.

I fear that the evangelical church on the whole has become too comfortable with God. I know that I have. I too easily slip into my easy chair in the morning with my cup of coffee and treat the Lion of Judah as if He were no threat whatsoever. As if He were in His own easy chair right beside me, happy to have been invited to mutually chat about what is going on. As if I were doing Him some kind of favor by checking in before the day begins. A.W. Tozer puts it like this,

The God of Abraham whom our fathers knew has withdrawn His conscious presence from us, and another God whom our fathers knew not is making himself at home among us. This God we have made and because we have made him we can understand him; because we have created him he can never surprise us, never overwhelm us, nor astonish us nor transcend us.

Amen.

I have been greatly challenged in this regard by the words of Stephen Charnock, Puritan pastor and theologian:

God is a Spirit infinitely happy, therefore we must approach him with cheerfulness; he is a Spirit of infinite majesty, therefore we must come before him with reverence; he is a Spirit infinitely high, therefore we must offer up our sacrifices with deepest humility; he is a Spirit infinitely holy, therefore we must address him with purity; he is a Spirit glorious, we therefore must acknowledge his excellency...he is a Spirit infinitely provoked by us, therefore we must offer up our worship in the name of a pacifying mediator and intercessor.

May God grant us the grace to approach Him in worship in the only way truly befitting of Who He is—face down.

FLASHPOINT
Worship is fundamentally a face down affair.

The Importance of Looking Upward

"They looked to Him and were radiant, and their faces were not ashamed." Ps.34:5

There are a thousand ills in our lives that can only be cured by worship. Our fears, addictions, jealousies, resentments, doubts, etc. normally remain stubbornly intact when our primary focus is on them and how to get rid of them. Now certainly there is an important time and place for looking honestly at our issues. But change ultimately comes not from looking within but from looking above. According to this passage, saints only become radiant when their faces are turned away from themselves and their struggles to a far more spectacular and compelling vista— God Himself. William Temple, former Archbishop of Canterbury, put it so well:

> *Both for perplexity and for dulled conscience the remedy is the same; sincere and spiritual worship. For worship is the submission of all our nature to God. It is the quickening of conscience by His holiness; the nourishment of mind with His truth; the purifying of imagination by His beauty; the opening of the heart to His love; the surrender of will to His purpose—and all of this gathered up in adoration, the most selfless emotion of which our nature is capable and therefore the chief remedy for that self-centeredness which is our original sin and the source of all actual*

sin. Yes—worship in spirit and truth is the way to the solution of perplexity and to the liberation from sin.

Please don't pass over his words too quickly. Mull over them, for they are filled with gems of life-changing truth. And most of all, they are a critical reminder that we are changed most powerfully by becoming awe-struck with God, rather than vainly trying to tinker with ourselves.

This is exactly the message of Paul, *"But we all, with unveiled face, beholding as in a mirror the glory of the Lord, are being transformed into the same image from glory to glory, just as by the Spirit of the Lord."* II Cor. 3:18 Notice the order: it is through *"beholding"* that we *"are being transformed."* (lit."transfigured"). Beholding what? Notice what Paul does not say. Through beholding our sin. Through beholding our wounds. Through beholding our responsibilities. Through beholding our circumstances. Though there is a time and place for each of these, the only vista powerful enough to change the deep parts within us is, as Paul says, *"the glory of the Lord."* The glory of God is His spectacular-ness, His weightiness, His off-the-chartness. A.W. Tozer puts it so well:

While we are looking at God we do not see ourselves—blessed riddance. The man who has struggled to purify himself and has had nothing but repeated failures will experience real relief when he stops tinkering with his soul and looks away to the perfect One. While he looks at Christ the very things he has so long been trying to do will be getting done within him. It will be God working in him to will and to do.

Amen!

> **FLASHPOINT**
> It is the look upward that most powerfully affects the change inward.

The Hearth

FIRE'S HOMESTEAD

"...concerning His Son Jesus Christ our Lord, who was born of the seed of David according to the flesh, and declared to be the Son of God with power according to the Spirit of holiness, by the resurrection from the dead."

– ROM. 1:3-4 –

"Remember Jesus Christ, having been raised from the dead, of the seed of David according to my gospel,"

– II TIM. 2:8 –

In many homes throughout history, the hearth has been the center of the house. Not only was it often physically the very mid-point of the family dwelling, it was also the center of family life. It was there that meals were cooked, books were read, guests were entertained, devotions were held, and a myriad of other family activities took place. It was within the secure confines of the two sides of the hearth that fire could burn most safely and beneficially.

Christianity has its own hearth, as it were. There are two vital realities which serve as the two sides between which the fires of true spirituality and deepening faith occur. Without these, there simply is no faith, no hope, no fire. End of game, everyone go home. But because of these, thousands upon thousands of Christians have given up their lives in blood, have turned their backs on this fleeting world and abandoned themselves to that King and kingdom which will never disappoint or fade away. The two realities? Christmas and Easter. More specifically, what Christmas and Easter represent.

Christmas celebrates the mind-numbing, heart-ravishing entrance of God into human history through the womb of a Jewish teenage peasant girl. Easter celebrates the resurrection from the dead of a Galilean carpenter turned rabbi turned Savior. Tragically, in our culture these two events are treated like grandmother's fine china. They brought down once a year, dusted off, and then put back safely until next year. Nothing, but nothing could be farther from God's intended purposes for these two bookends of dynamic, vital *spirituality. These are 365 days a year remembrances, and the entirety of our Christian lives must, must be spent going deeper and deeper into these two wildly improbable realities. These meditations are devoted to the significance of Christmas and Easter every day of our lives. As well there are a few devoted to the human kindling for God's hearth—brokenness, humility, and dependency.*

Christmas Wonder

"For unto us a Child is born, unto us a Son is given; and the government will be upon His shoulder. And His name will be called Wonderful..." Is.9:6

Ultimately, what nourishes and sustains our spiritual lives over the long haul is not *discipline,* but *wonder.* Certainly discipline is a vital part of discipleship; this need never be negated. Wonder without discipline ultimately leads to unrealized potential. But discipline without wonder inevitably results in unimpassioned duty. It degenerates into dry, barren, rule-keeping, what C. John Miller has aptly described as *"joyless moralism."*

Wonder, surprise, astonishment, etc. are the endorphins of true spirituality. They release new energy into the bloodstream of vital, dynamic Christianity. The only Christianity, by the way, which is worth having. And for sure, worth marketing. And if Christmas means anything, it means surprise and wonder. The Hebrew word translated *"Wonderful"* in this passage carries more the idea *"astonishing, stunning"* etc. Interesting that this is the first title given our Lord. J.B. Phillips, the Anglican clergyman noted for his translation of the New Testament puts it so well:

> *If New Testament Christianity is to reappear today with its power and joy and courage, men must recapture the basic conviction that this is a Visited planet. It is not enough to express formal belief in the "Incarnation" or in the "Divinity of Christ"; the staggering truth must be accepted afresh—that in this vast, mysterious universe, of which we are an almost infinitesimal part, the great Mystery, Whom we call God, has visited our planet in Person. It is from this conviction that there springs unconquerable certainty and unquenchable faith and hope. It is not enough to believe theoretically that Jesus was both God and Man; not enough to admire, respect, and even worship Him; it is not even enough to try to follow Him. The reason for the insufficiency of these things is that the modern intelligent mind, which has had its horizons widened in dozens of different ways, has got to be shocked afresh by the audacious central Fact—that, as a sober matter of history, God became one of us.*

Imagine the astonishment of the angels as they watched:

- Mary change God's diaper.
- The Bread of Life being fed.
- God learning to walk. Imagine the Provider of all strength having to pick Himself up and try again!
- God learning to talk. Mary, what was it like to teach the Incarnate Word how to pronounce Jehovah?
- God being washed by one in need of His washing.
- The Creator of the universe learning how to set the table. God Almighty learning how to sit up straight. When Jesus said the blessing did it occur to anyone that he really was talking to His Father?
- The Maker of all things learning the skills of carpentry. Joseph, did it take you long to teach God where to put his tools when he was finished?
- The Redeemer of mankind learning how to hold a hammer and drive in nails. When did He first begin to realize…?
- The One Who chose us being chosen for a neighborhood game of tag. John, what was it like to tell God that He was out?

You get the picture. *"And the Word became flesh and dwelt among us…"* (Jn. 1:14) is far more than an historical event. It is one of the most stunning, mind-blowing, soul-ravishing realities our faith has to offer. May God grant that we never get over it.

> **FLASHPOINT**
> Christmas was never meant to be
> recovered from.

The True Bond of Christmas

"The book of the genealogy of Jesus Christ, the Son of David, the Son of Abraham:...Judah begot Perez and Zerah by Tamar,...Salmon begot Boaz by Rahab, Boaz begot Obed by Ruth...David the king begot Solomon by her who had been the wife of Uriah...And Jacob begot Joseph the husband of Mary, of whom was born Jesus who is called Christ." Matt.1:1-16

The gospel of Matthew was written to a Jewish audience with the intent of demonstrating that Jesus of Nazareth was indeed the awaited Messiah, rightful Heir of the throne of David. For the Jews, pedigree was not important...it was absolutely crucial. Thus–very understandably—Matthew begins by a detailed genealogy of Jesus Christ as both the Son of David and the Son Abraham.

This *had* to be established before he could go any further.

What isn't so understandable is why five women are included in the account. There was no compelling, historical need for their names to be included. What isn't so understandable is why at least three, if not four, were Gentiles, considered social outcasts at the time. What isn't so understandable is why three of them had less than stellar reputations. What isn't so understandable is why two of them—Tamar and Rahab—engaged in prostitution. What isn't so understandable is why one of them engaged in prostitution as a way of life. Why in the world choose these women to help prove the royal blood of the Messiah? For that matter, when was the last time you heard of a daughter named Bathsheba, Tamar, or Rahab?

Fact of the matter is that *grace is never understandable.* The people God reaches out to and works through in this world are the broken, desperate, and foolish (I Cor.1:26-29). Broken enough to fully recognize and embrace their own sinfulness. Desperate enough to give up their own idolatrous strongholds and flee to the Rock that is higher than them. Foolish enough to simply take God at His word. Foolish enough to trust in His simple, naked promise of forgiveness and restoration.

Indeed, the recorded genealogy of Jesus Christ provides hope of stunning proportions. Hope that no failure need be final. Hope that God eagerly invites wayward sons and daughters back to the banquet table of restored, vital intimacy with Him. Hope that He uses only one kind of person to accomplish His work through—those who have failed. *He simply has no other material to work with.* And so maybe it's a bit more understandable why Matthew, the former tax collector, included these women in his genealogy. Radically forgiven sinners feel a special bond with other radically forgiven sinners. And if we even remotely know ourselves, we too will join him in that same bond. The true bond of Christmas.

> **FLASHPOINT**
> Christmas reminds us that Christ came for everyone, including those who have failed. No, *especially* those who have failed...all of us.

Regaining the Wonder

"And without controversy great is the mystery of godliness: God was manifested in the flesh..." I Tim. 3:16

The greatest tragedy of Christmas is not commercialism. It is familiarity. The reality of God invading human history with an umbilical cord and a need for mother's milk no longer startles us. We have become wholly at ease with the mystery Paul asserts as *"great."* One of the most eloquent rebuttals to this loss of amazement I have ever seen came from a commentary Harry Reasoner made in 1971 as he closed out "60 Minutes":

> *The basis for this tremendous burst of buying things and gift giving and parties and near hysteria, is a quiet event that Christians believe actually happened a long time ago. You can say that in all societies there has always been a midwinter festival, and that many of the trappings of our Christmas are almost violently pagan, but you come back to the central fact of the day, ...the birth of God on earth.*
>
> *It leaves you only three ways of accepting Christmas.*
>
> *One is cynically, as a time to make money or endorse the making of it.*
>
> *One is graciously, the appropriate attitude for non-Christians, who wish their fellow citizens all the joys their beliefs entitle them. And the third, of course, is reverently.*
>
> *If this is the anniversary of the appearance of the Lord of the universe in the form of a helpless babe—it is a very important day. It's a startling idea, of course, the whole story that a virgin was selected by God to bear His Son as a way of showing His love and concern for man. It's my guess that, in spite of all the lip service given to it, it is not an idea that has been popular with theologians.*

It's a somewhat illogical idea, and theologians like logic almost as much as they like God. It's so revolutionary an idea that it probably could only have come from a God that is beyond logic, and beyond theology. It has a magnificent appeal. Almost nobody has seen God, and almost nobody has any real idea of what He is like, and the truth is that among men the idea of seeing God suddenly, and standing in a very bright light, is not necessarily a completely comforting and appealing idea. But everyone has seen babies, and most people like them. If God wanted to be loved as well as feared, He moved correctly here, for a baby grows up and learns all about people. If God wanted to be intimately a part of Man he moved correctly, for the experience of birth and family-hood is our most intimate and precious experience.

So it comes beyond logic. It is either a falsehood or it is the truest thing in the world. It's the story of the great innocence of God the baby. God in the person of man has such a dramatic shock toward the heart, that it, if it is not true, for Christians, nothing is true. So even if you have not got your shopping all done and are swamped with the commercialism and the frenzy, be at peace...The story stands.

So, if a Christian is touched only once a year, the touching is still worth it, and maybe on some given Christmas, some final quiet morning, the touch will take.

Here's praying that the touch will take in all our lives... and that the amazement will remain all year long. Nothing could make for a better Christmas.

> **FLASHPOINT**
> Let the wonder of Christmas linger...
> all year long.

The Danger of Easter

"And if Christ is not risen, then our preaching is in vain, and your faith is also in vain." I Cor.15:14

Easter is possibly the brightest, cheeriest, and most wholly unthreatening holiday of the year. It is a co-op between the Easter bunny and Jesus Christ. Sometimes it's hard to figure out who gets top billing. Easter dresses, Easter eggs, Easter lunches, and sunrise Easter services all lend a hand to make this such a pleasant day for families.

But we do well to stop and remember something else about Easter. Because of Easter:

Peter was crucified upside down around 68 A.D.

James the son of Zebedee was put to death by Herod Agrippa I shortly before the day of the Passover.

Andrew is reported to have been crucified at Patrae in Achaia.

Philip was executed at Hierapolis.

Bartholomew was martyred in India.

Matthew was martyred in Ethiopia.

Thomas was lanced through in Ethiopia

James, son of Alpheus, was thrown down from the temple by the scribes and Pharisees. He was then stoned, and his brains dashed out with a fuller's club.

Simon the Zealot was martyred.

Paul was beheaded.

For these men, and countless others throughout history, the resurrection proved beyond all doubt that the claims of Jesus of Nazareth are *true*. And because they are true, they are worth living for. And dying for. And Easter, wonderful as it is reminds us that our faith is far more than a bright, cheery optimism to make life more tolerable. Our faith is truth-riddled. It is founded upon an actual, historical, grave-snatching event 2,000 years ago. It is confirmed by the mangled bodies and bloodshed of those who actually saw the resurrected Christ. And it requires that we approach Easter in a radically different way than the rest of our culture. That we leave mindless cheeriness to the Easter Bunny and bring to Jesus what He deserves—awestruck worship, authentic spirituality, and radical, risk-taking discipleship. All based on truth, of course.

> **FLASHPOINT**
> Easter is the reason untold thousands of
> believers have laid down their lives in blood.
> It is also the reason we should give up our
> lives to Christ in faith.

Because It's True

"...he preached to them Jesus and the resurrection." Acts
17:18

I've never forgotten it. A number of years ago I was listening to a message by John Stott when he posed the question, *"What's the primary reason we should share the gospel with
others?"* He then gave everyone a moment to answer the
question for themselves. I thought of things like "people
need to hear so they can be saved and escape hell," "the
gospel alone can truly transform peoples' lives," etc.

Then he quietly, but very, very powerfully stated, *"The
primary reason we share the gospel is that it is true."* He then
went on to note that it just so happens that the gospel *is*
good news for many, many reasons. But even if it weren't

good news—but still true—we owe the world a chance to hear its message. And those words have continued to ring in my ears to this day.

And for me personally, that's perhaps the most important part of Easter. It reminds us that the most important aspect of the gospel is not that it brings us *happiness* or *comfort,* but *truth.* C.S. Lewis was once asked which religion of the world provides the most happiness. I love his response:

While it lasts, the religion of worshipping oneself is the best... As you perhaps know, I haven't always been a Christian. I didn't go to religion to make me happy. I always knew a bottle of Port would do that. If you want a religion to make you feel really comfortable, I certainly don't recommend Christianity. I am certain there must be a patent American article on the market which will suit you far better, but I can't give any advice on it.

Lewis became a follower of Christ because of one overriding, irrefutable, inescapable reason—it was true, not that it was comfortable. In fact, it was anything but comfortable for him:

You must picture me alone in that room in Magdalen, night after night, feeling, whenever my mind lifted even for a second from my work, the steady, unrelenting approach of Him whom I so earnestly desired not to meet. That which I greatly feared had at last come upon me. In the Trinity Term of 1929 I gave in, and admitted that God was God, and knelt and prayed: perhaps, that night, the most dejected and reluctant convert in all England.

And the resurrection of Christ was one of the most central reasons for his conversion.

Malcolm Muggeridge, the famed British journalist, spent most of his life as an agnostic. Yet through his study of the resurrection he ultimately became a Christ-follower. He writes in his work "Jesus: The Man Who Lives:"

> *The coming of Jesus into the world is the most stupendous event in human history....*
>
> *What is unique about Jesus is that, on the testimony and in the experience of innumerable people, of all sorts and conditions, of all races and nationalities from the simplest and most primitive to the most sophisticated and cultivated, he remains alive.*
>
> *That the Resurrection happened... seems to be indubitably true.*
>
> *Either Jesus never was or he still is....with the utmost certainty, I assert he still is.*

And so, as we approach Easter, we do well to remember that its primary purpose is not to make us comfortable or even happy. It's to remind us that an actual, historical, unrepeatable event is the unfailing bedrock of our faith. And that apart from it...a bottle of Port is really about all we're left with to handle life.

> **FLASHPOINT**
> The empty tomb is our faith's nuclear blast. Nothing more explosively confirms the truth of Christianity than a risen Savior.

Growing in Humility

"For I am the least of the apostles, unworthy to be called an apostle…" I Cor. 15:9

"To me, who am less than the least of all the saints, this grace was given…" Eph. 3:8

"This is a faithful saying and worthy of all acceptance, that Christ Jesus came into the world to save sinners, of whom I am chief." I Tim. 1:15

Did you catch the sequence? *"…least of the apostles…least of all the saints…chief of sinners."* Paul descends from least of the apostles to least of the saints to the worst of sinners. Did you catch the chronology? Each letter is written later than the previous one. I Cor. around 56 A.D., Ephesians around 60 A.D., and I Timothy around 64 A.D. So what's the point?

Very simply, it is this. Paul saw his sin more, not less, as he matured. As we are growing in Christ, we should be increasing in the humbled awareness of how desperately sinful we still remain. Though our sin does not define us as believers (II Cor. 5:17), it remains a very real and active part of our entire make-up. And the closer we get to Christ, the more profoundly aware we become of the how desperately far short we fall of His perfection. At all times. In all circumstances. We see more and more clearly that even the right things we do are still tainted with many subtle forms of self-glorying and self-dependency that eluded our observation in earlier days of our faith. C.S. Lewis wrote, *"For [Alexander Whyte], one essential symptom of the regenerate life is a permanent, and permanently horrified, perception of one's natural and (it seems) unalterable corruption. The true Christian's nostril is to be continually attentive to the inner cesspool."*

Jonathan Edwards writes in "Personal Narrative:"

Often, since I lived in this town, I have had very affecting views of my own sinfulness and vileness; very frequently to such a degree as to hold me in a kind of loud weeping, sometimes for a considerable time together; so that I have often been forced to shut myself up. I have had a vastly greater sense of my own wickedness, and the badness of my heart, than ever I had before my conversion. It has often appeared to me, that if God should mark iniquity against me, I should appear the very worst of all mankind... When I look into my heart, and take a view of my wickedness, it looks like an abyss infinitely deeper than hell.

I love J.I. Packer's take on statements such as these. He notes either, "[Puritans] *were very wicked men or we are very superficial Christians.*" He is right on both counts. Only they were no more wicked than any of us. They just knew themselves better. I say it again, as we are growing in Christ we should be increasing in the humbled awareness of how desperately sinful we still remain. If not, something is desperately wrong.

But if we *only* grow in awareness of our sin, something else is desperately wrong. God doesn't reveal our sin to make us feel bad, but needy. Desperately needy. Needy for forgiveness we cannot provide for ourselves. Needy for victory over sin we cannot provide for ourselves. Therefore, deepened sin awareness should always lead to heightened cross appreciation. Ultimately what should overwhelm us as believers is not the staggering immensity of our sin, but the even more staggering magnitude of our forgiveness. As well, our sin awareness should lead to new depths of resource dependency. Dependency on divine, supernatural resources—our only hope for overcoming the sin which nips at our heels all day long.

May God bless you, my fellow struggler. Keep your eyes firmly fixed on Christ. Yet don't avert your eyes from the sin He points out. But most of all, gaze incessantly upon the cross—we need it every hour. No, every second. And the more we grow, the more we realize it.

> **FLASHPOINT**
> Depth awareness of our sin is the prerequisite for heightened gratitude for the cross.

What We Never Outgrow

"I will go in the strength of the Lord GOD; I will make mention of Your righteousness, of Yours only. O God, You have taught me from my youth; and to this day I declare Your wondrous works. Now also when I am old and grayheaded, O God, do not forsake me, until I declare Your strength to this generation, Your power to everyone who is to come." Ps.71:16-18

The Psalmist is an old man. By his own admission he notes, *"Now also when I am old and grayheaded..."*. He was once young. He remembers those days well—*"O God, You have taught me from my youth..."* But days of youth are gone forever and what remains in their place are the myriads of lessons God *"taught"* him over the years. Lessons on patience. On courage. On forgiveness. On failure. On loving God with one's entire being. The psalmist has grown and matured much over the years.

But though he has *grown*, there is something he has not *outgrown*. And never would. That something is dependency. Radical, naked, desperate dependency upon God for every good in his life. *Maturity brings no exemptions from neediness. "I will go in the strength of the Lord God..."* Those words constitute our sole hope whether early in life or late. At age 85, Caleb (one of the greatest saints of the Bible) notes, "... *It may be that the Lord will be with me, and I shall be able to drive them out as the Lord said"* (Josh. 14:12). This aged man of God recognized that any hope of success was grounded in *"...the Lord will be with me."* Truly, maturity brings no exemptions from neediness or downgrades in dependency.

British pastor F.B. Meyer puts it so well, *"There is nothing small in the Christian life—nothing so small that we can combat it in our own strength. Apart from God, the smallest temptations will be more than a match for us...The victories which we have won in fellowship with God have imparted no inherent might to us; we are as weak as ever. And when directly we are brought into collision with the least of our enemies, apart from Him, we will inevitably go down before the shock."*

I love his thought, *"The victories which we have won in fellowship with God have imparted no inherent might to us; we are as weak as ever."* How, how true! Past victories do not infuse us with extra strength for the future. Overcoming sin can subtly tempt us to believe that somehow we are outgrowing dependency. Nothing could be farther from reality. As Meyer puts it, *"...we are weak as ever."* Beyond that, only those who go about *"in the strength of the Lord God"* are the ones who *"make mention of Your righteousness, of Yours only."* They alone are the ones whose message is utterly God-riveted: *"I declare Your wondrous works... I declare Your strength to this generation, Your power to everyone who is to come."* There is the closest possible connection between tasting God's power personally and the compulsion to proclaim God's greatness passionately. No matter what stage of life.

> **FLASHPOINT**
> Past successes in the spiritual life do not exempt us from radical dependency upon resurrection power for today.

Led To Humility

"And you shall remember that the LORD your God led you all the way these forty years in the wilderness, to humble you...So He humbled you," Dt. 8:2-3

I wonder if this is not the ultimate end of all God's dealings with us in this life. To humble us...to bring us to the end of ourselves. In reality, it is the greatest favor He can do for us. Until then we will be too confident, too self-reliant, too impressed with ourselves to be able to experience His best. So how is this critical commodity of brokenness best developed? In a word, true humility is never brought about by focusing primarily on our own sinfulness, but upon the stunning greatness and glory of Another. When Isaiah *"saw the Lord sitting on a throne, high and lifted up..."* (Is.6:1), he became keenly aware of his own sinfulness in ways that he had not previously seen. *"So I said, 'Woe is me, for I am undone! Because I am a man of unclean lips, and I dwell in the midst of a people of unclean lips; for my eyes have seen the King, the Lord of Hosts"* (Is.6:5 emphasis mine).

When he caught a glimpse of the radiant, stunning glory of God, he recognized that he was not all that different from the very people he had just been condemning (Rom.2:1-3). "...I dwell *in the midst* of a people of unclean lips..." is the heart cry of every genuinely broken saint. The air in one's house appears clear until a sunbeam makes its entrance. Then in the bright light of that ray we see all kinds of particles of dust for the first time. We can never see those particles apart from the sun.

In the same way, the depths of our sin remain hidden until seen in the light of the Son. Phillips Brooks said, *"The true way to be humble is not to stoop until you are smaller than yourself, but to stand at your real height against some higher nature that will show you what the real smallness of your greatness is."* I love that thought.

Pride is not a minor imperfection in God's children. It is a fatal disease. Howard E. Butt, founder of HEB food stores, puts it so well in his article, "The Art of Being a Big Shot":

It is my pride that makes me independent of God. It's appealing to me to feel that I am the master of my fate, that I run my own life, call my own shots, go it alone. But, that feeling is my basic dishonesty. I can't go it alone. I have to get help from other people, and I can't ultimately rely on myself. I'm dependent on God for my very next breath. It is dishonest of me to pretend that I'm anything but a man—small, weak, and limited. So, living independent of God is self-delusion. It is not just a matter of pride being an unfortunate little trait, and humility being an attractive little virtue; it's my inner psychological integrity that's at stake. When I am conceited, I am lying to myself about what I am. I am pretending to be God, and not man. My pride is the idolatrous worship of myself. And that is the national religion of Hell!

I love his phrase, "*It is not just a matter of pride being an unfortunate little trait, and humility being an attractive little virtue...*" So, so true. Pride is, in fact, a really big deal to God. So is humility. And hopefully it is to us as well.

> **FLASHPOINT**
> Major in humility. It lays the groundwork for everything else.

Sparks
FIRE'S EMISSARIES

"It only takes a spark to get a fire going…"
So goes the campfire song, originally composed as
a hymn under the title "Pass It On" by Kurt Kaiser
in 1969. Believe it or not, the song sparked controversy
among some of the older saints for being too
worldly and borrowing from the devil's music!
Probably best that most of them aren't around
to hear today's Christian music…

But the fact of the matter is it only takes a spark to ignite a fire of enormous proportions. As James tells us, "See how great a forest a little fire kindles" *Jas. 3:5.* We have all seen the pictures of the devastating fires in California and the wildfires of West Texas. Hundreds of thousands of acres consumed because of an unchecked campfire, a smoldering ember, or a wayward spark.

In the kingdom of God, some of the greatest movements of the Spirit's fire have been kindled by a single, obscure saint. Or a quiet, unheralded act of faithfulness. From the unpretentious giving of the widow's mite to effects like Sunday school teacher Edward Kimball's quiet influence on the powerful evangelist D.L. Moody, it truly only takes a spark to get a fire going. A faltering spark. An imperfect spark. An often forgotten spark. But a spark nonetheless, and the history of the church is never the same.

I like to call sparks "fire's emissaries." They aren't the fire; they are only the "sent forth ones" from the fire. But oh what a difference they can make! These devotionals focus on two primary themes. First of all, it costs to be a spark. No way around it. Secondly, sparks have far greater influence than anyone can imagine because God takes responsibility for keeping the fire going. "A little one shall become a thousand, and a small one a strong nation. I, the LORD, will hasten it in its time" *(Is. 60:22).*

The Power of Obscure Obedience

"And He looked up and saw the rich putting their gifts into the treasury, and He saw also a certain poor widow putting in two mites. So He said, 'Truly I say to you that this poor widow has put in more than all; for all these out of their abundance have put in offerings for God, but she out of her poverty put in all the livelihood that she had.'" Lk.21:1-4

It was her crowning moment. The day that would ensure she would be forever remembered in the pages of scripture. The hour of her great obedience. Only she never knew it. And never would in this life.

Compelled by her love for God and desire to please Him, she gave beyond what was prudent for a poor widow. Unlike the Pharisees, she didn't look around to see who was watching. She just gave and went her way, oblivious to the ramifications of her quiet, humble obedience. Her gift of two mites (not a tithe, by the way) may not have seemed like much to the temple crowd that day. But our Lord saw it differently. Very differently. And said so in no uncertain terms. *"Truly I say to you that this poor widow has put in more than all; for all these out of their abundance have put in offerings for God, but she out of her poverty put in all the livelihood that she had."* From that day forth this unnamed, obscure widow would become an example par excellence of the kind of giving which catches our Lord's attention. But again, she would never know that until she hit heaven.

Think with me for just a moment. Suppose this widow

had been the wealthiest woman in Israel. In fact, suppose she had control over all the money in Israel at the time. And suppose she had taken every last shekel and given it to the temple. Would that amount come even remotely close to the money which has been given over the last 2,000 years because of her example? How many sermons in the past 2,000 years have been preached on her? How many hands have dug deeper into their wallets than they normally would have because her inspiration? Of course there is no way to prove it, but I am absolutely convinced that far more money has been given as a result of her obscure obedience than was even available at the time of Christ.

Never underestimate the power of obscure obedience. She had no idea what her routine, unheralded, oblivious obedience would lead to. And neither do you or I. Oswald Chambers put it well,

> *We can all do the heroic thing, but can we live in the drab humiliating valley where there is nothing amazing, but mostly disaster, certainly humiliation, and emphatically everything drab and dull and lowly? This is where Jesus Christ lived most of His life.*

I say it again. Never underestimate the power of obscure obedience. Even in the valley. No, especially in the valley.

FLASHPOINT
It is ours to toss the pebble into the pond.
It is God's to keep the ripples going.

Tasting the Best

"But none of these things move me; nor do I count my life dear to myself, so that I may finish my race with joy, and the ministry which I received from the Lord Jesus, to testify to the gospel of the grace of God." Acts 20:24

According to Paul, he had only two choices. He could either *"count my life dear to myself"* or he could *"finish my course with joy."* He could coddle his life and seek to insulate it from discomfort, danger, and trouble. Or he could throw caution to the wind, and abandon himself to the highly dangerous but equally joy-riddled enterprise *"to testify of the gospel of the grace of God."* But he couldn't have both.

The grave danger of settling for safety and comfort as one's highest aspiration in life is not that it makes us soft. It's that it makes us paupers. It robs us of the best God has designed for us. And far worse, it robs God of the potential glory our lives could have garnished Him. During his last visit back to England, the notable explorer and missionary David Livingstone spoke to the students at Cambridge University. In his address he spoke these words concerning the sacrifices he had made during his years in Africa:

> For my own part, I have never ceased to rejoice that God has appointed me to such an office. People talk about the sacrifice I have made in spending so much of my life in Africa. Can that be called a sacrifice which is simply paid back as a small part of a great debt owing to our God, which we can never repay? Is that

a sacrifice which brings its own blest reward in healthful activity, the consciousness of doing good, peace of mind, and a bright hope of a glorious destiny hereafter? Away with the word in such a view, and with such a thought! It is emphatically no sacrifice. Say rather it is a privilege. Anxiety, sickness, suffering, or danger, now and then, with a foregoing of common conveniences and charities of this life, may make us pause, and cause the spirit to waver, and the soul to sink; but let this only be for a moment. All these are nothing when compared with the glory which shall be revealed in and for us. I never made a sacrifice.

Though Livingstone had been mauled by a lion, suffered innumerable sicknesses and bites, and worked in almost constant jeopardy of his life, none of these things were what he remembered primarily about his years in Africa. In his words, *"I never made a sacrifice."* He tasted the vibrant rest and high adventure of white water Christianity; a life lived with the floodgates wide open. And that overshadows everything. Especially safety.

> **FLASHPOINT**
> We are called to empty our hands so we can seize hold of God's best for us.

The Disruptive Call of God

"By faith Abraham obeyed when he was called to go out to the place which he would receive as an inheritance. And he went out, not knowing where he was going." Heb. 11:8

A close walk with God will inevitably be hazardous at times. Hazardous to what we believe is best for us. Hazardous to our beliefs of where we can best serve God. Being used by God sooner or later turns one's world upside down. Just ask Abraham. Deeply rooted in affluence, dwelling comfortably in Ur of the Chaldees, his life would be sandblasted by the unsolicited call of God. So would Sarah's. And neither of them would ever be the same. This is unspeakably fortunate for us and millions of others, whose lives have been profoundly impacted by their radical response to God's highly inconvenient calling upon their lives.

And he went out, not knowing where he was going. God does not provide MapQuest for his saints so that they can be sure to understand the whole path of their pilgrimage here. Almost always He provides only one thing—*the very next step.* Not the next two steps. Not the next three steps. And like Abraham, He calls us to take the next step wholly blind as to the next step that will follow. The old Franciscan prayer puts it so well,

Lord, take me where You want me to go;
Let me meet who you want me to meet,

Tell me what You want me to say,
And then keep me out of the way.

Samuel Chadwick, an early Methodist preacher put it like this:

We are moved by the act of God. Omniscience holds no confer-
ence. Infinite authority leaves no room for compromise. Eternal
love offers no explanations. The Lord expects to be trusted. He
disturbs us at will. Human arrangements are disregarded, family
ties ignored, business claims put aside. We are never asked if it
is convenient…

I'm especially struck by his last statement, *"We are never asked if it is convenient."* I think Abraham and Sarah would echo a hearty *"amen"* to that statement. So would David Livingstone, William Carey, Hudson Taylor, and a host of fragrant saints throughout the centuries who discovered first-hand a vital truth: Temporal convenience and eternal significance rarely go hand in hand. God's best for our lives comes at a cost. Often a high one. But one which will pale in comparison to the supernatural joy and deep satisfaction of having taken God-ordained risks in a play-safe world. And making an eternal difference during our short stay on this earth. Just ask Abraham.

> **FLASHPOINT**
> One cannot play safe and be a difference maker at the same time.

Influencing Our Own Street Corner

"The woman then left her waterpot, went her way into the city, and said to the men, 'Come, see a Man who told me all things that I ever did. Could this be the Christ?'"
Jn. 4:28-29

We all are the Samaritan woman. Every one of us. No exceptions. We all have our city. Every one of us. No exceptions. And we all have the same calling. Every one of us. No exceptions. Let me explain.

We are all sinners saved by the same grace that transformed this woman of Samaria so many years ago. Did she need more grace than most of us? I think not. No, I *know* not. Fact is, all of our lives are as pock-marked by sin as hers was. Our sins may be more respectable, more refined, more tolerated by the Christian community (judgmentalism, name dropping, self-promoting, coveting, etc.), but no less sin. In fact, maybe even more. I love the way the missionary Bishop Moule expressed it in his commentary on Romans,

> *The harlot, the liar, the murderer, are short of it [God's glory] but so are you. Perhaps they stand at the bottom of a mine, and you on the crest of the Alps; but you are as little able to touch the stars as they are.*

So, so true. Everyone of us has slept around just as much as that Samaritan woman ever thought of. The only difference being that we have uncovered ourselves to the gods of this world and made love to the created rather than the Creator (Is. 57:7-8). But we have no less sinned.

We all have our city. Everyone of us has a natural sphere of influence where we spend most of our time—job, neighborhood, school, etc. Did that sphere of influence come by accident? No, a thousand times no! Your sphere of influence...my sphere of influence...all have been carefully crafted by the skilled hand of an infinitely wise and sovereign God. Our circle of influence is not coincidental, it is divinely orchestrated.

We all have the same calling. It is not to escape our natural sphere of influence to go out and find other ministry. Jesus told the formerly demon-possessed man who wanted to travel with Him, *"Go home to your friends, and tell them what great things the Lord has done for you, and how He has had compassion on you."* (Mk. 5:19) Certainly there will be

ministry opportunities outside our natural sphere of influence. But these can never, should never, must never re-
place the premier mission field God has deployed each of
us to—like Jesus's encounter with the Samaritan woman
at the well at Sychar, our own Sychar. And our calling is
not to judge, nor rebuke, nor even so much to change our
Sychar. It is to invite. It is to point out. It is to draw attention away from ourselves and say to those around us in
a respectful, though urgent way—*"Come see a Man...Could
this be the Christ?"* It is to spend our days as graced beggars
telling other beggars where they can find bread. Especially
those on our own street corner.

> **FLASHPOINT**
> Our influence for Christ must begin on our
> own street corner.

The Unknown End of Faithfulness

"'The glory of this latter temple shall be greater than the former', says the Lord of Hosts. And in this place I shall give peace..." Haggai 2:9

One of the great problems with focusing preeminently upon present results is that they so often represent only part of the story. And not infrequently, the part of the story that is left out is monumentally the most important. As in Haggai's day.

Who, but who, would ever have dreamed that the present temple being constructed would one day garner more glory for God than Solomon's? Could the people of Haggai's day possibly have known that one day the very Son of God Himself would walk and talk within the confines of the temple they were working on? I'm quite certain that this possibility never crossed the minds of any of the workers. Fortunately, God spoke to them before they threw in the towel. And fortunately for us, we learn a tremendous lesson from their day. We have no idea how far God can take our smallest act of faithfulness. Consider the following example of this from Crosswalk:

Perhaps you've heard of the chain of events that began when an everyday, garden-variety man named Edward Kimball made himself available to God. Gripped by a sense of urgency when he learned he had little time left to live, Kimball reached out to the young men in his Sunday School class. One of them was a young shoe clerk, and Kimball led him to Christ in the back room of the store. That man was D. L. Moody, who became one of the great evangelists of the 19th century. On a trip to the British Isles, Moody's ministry impacted the life of a young pastor named Frederick Meyer, who later traveled to America and preached in Moody's school in Massachusetts. His message changed the entire ministry of another young preacher named J. Wilbur Chapman. Chapman went on to become one of the most effective evangelists of his time. He eventually turned his ministry over to a YMCA clerk who had been serving as his advance man to set up his crusades. He had no formal training, but Billy Sunday had learned to preach by watching Chapman. He led hundreds of thousands to Christ in the early part of the 20th century as he preached in the largest cities in the nation. In 1924, Sunday conducted a series of meetings in Charlotte, North Carolina. Those meetings led to another city-wide evangelist outreach in 1932 led by Mordacai Ham. It was there that a young 16-year old baseball player made a decision to follow Christ. That 16-year old was Billy Graham.

The fascinating thing about all this is that Edward Kimball came very close to not sharing with Moody. In his own words,

I started down town to Holton's shoe store. When I was nearly there, I began to wonder whether I ought to go just then, during business hours. And I thought maybe my mission might embar-

rass the boy, that when I went away the other clerks might ask who I was, and when they learned might taunt Moody and ask if I was trying to make a good boy out of him. While I was pondering over it all, I passed the store without noticing it. Then when I found I had gone by the door, I determined to make a dash for it and have it over at once.

What a great line—"*I determined to make a dash for it and have it over.*" Maybe not the most perfectly motivated obedience, but obedience all the same.

What amazing things God can do with the smallest, faltering acts of faithfulness! Could Edward Kimball have had any idea that his little faithfulness would set off the spiritual avalanche that it did? Of course not. Nor do any of us know where our acts of faithfulness can lead.

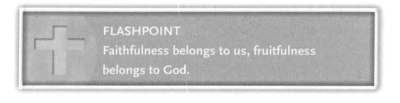

FLASHPOINT
Faithfulness belongs to us, fruitfulness belongs to God.

On the Way

"And Moses told his father-in-law all that the LORD had done to Pharaoh and to the Egyptians for Israel's sake, all the hardship that had come upon them on the way, and how the LORD had delivered them." Ex. 18:8

There are unique hardships that occur in our lives because—and only because we are *"on the way."* If Moses had chosen to avoid the call of God at the burning bush then he would never have *"told his father-in-law…all the hardship that had come upon them on the way, and how the LORD had delivered them."* He could have continued herding sheep for Jethro and enjoyed a safe, fairly comfortable existence. But once he responded to the radical call of God, he encountered a plethora of hardships. He exchanged comfort and safety for danger, heartaches, disappointments, betrayals, misunderstandings, criticisms, opposition, and weariness. Please read carefully the words of John Henry Jowett:

Now the range of our possible sufferings is determined by the largeness and nobility of our aims. It is possible to evade a multitude of sorrows by the cultivation of an insignificant life. Indeed, if it be a man's ambition to avoid the troubles of life, the receipt is perfectly simple—let him shed his ambitions in every direction, let him assiduously cultivate a little life, with the fewest correspondences and relations.

By this means a whole continent of afflictions will be escaped and will remain unknown. Cultivate negations, and large tracts of the universe will cease to exist. For instance, cultivate deafness and you are saved from the horrors of discord. Cultivate blindness, and you are saved from the assault of the ugly. Stupefy a sense, and you shut out a world.

And therefore, it is literally true that if you want to get through the world with the smallest trouble, you must reduce yourself to the smallest compass. And, indeed, that is why so many people, and even so many professedly Christian people, get through life so easily, and with a minimum acquaintance with tribulation. It is because they have reduced their souls to a minimum, that their course through the years is not so much the transit of a man, as the passage of an amoeba. They have no finely organized nervous system, or they have deadened and arrested the growth of one nerve after another. They have cut the sensitive wires which bind the individual to the race, and they are cozily self-contained, and the shuddering sorrow of the world never disturbs their seclusion.

Tiny souls can dodge through life; bigger souls are blocked on every side.

How amazingly well put! It costs to count, no way around it. Being *"on the way"* is not a path for the fainthearted. But it is only *"on the way"* that one also experiences the blatant power of God—*"all that the LORD had done to Pharaoh and to the Egyptians for Israel's sake."* It is only *"on the way"* that one tastes what it is to have God supernaturally provide—*"and how the LORD had delivered them."* And it is only *"on the way"*

that one's life can count for more than sheep. And count…
for all eternity.

> **FLASHPOINT**
> It costs to count. But the satisfaction lingers
> infinitely longer than the pain.

Pebble Tossing

*"I commend to you Phoebe our sister, who is a servant of
the church in Cenchrea…she has been a helper of many
and of myself also."* Rom. 16:1-2

Faithfulness belongs to us, fruitfulness belongs to God.
Or to put it another way, it is our part to toss down spiritual pebbles in Christ's strength from the top of our God-
assigned mountain. It is God's part to take the pebble and
create His own avalanche beyond our limited vision…which
is something He specializes in. *"A little one shall become a thousand, and a small one a strong nation. I, the LORD, will hasten it in
its time."* (Is. 60:22). Consider Phoebe for instance.

Paul describes her as *"a servant"* and *"a helper of many and
of myself also."* Simply put she was a faithful pebble-toss-

er, serving many in practical, Christ-scented ways. Little could she have known that one of the pebbles God enabled her to toss would result in an avalanche of unfathomable proportions. The pebble? Simply to hand-deliver a letter Paul had written to the saints in Rome. We know it today as the book of Romans. Could Phoebe have ever imagined in her wildest dreams...

...That in September of 386 a young philosopher would hear the words from a child, *"Take up and read"* while in his garden. Taking up the book of Romans he would read, *"Let us walk properly, as in the day, not in revelry and drunkenness, not in lewdness and lust, not in strife and envy. But put on the Lord Jesus Christ, and make no provision for the flesh, to fulfill its lusts."* (Rom. 13:13-14). That philosopher—Augustine—would be converted right on the spot. He would also become one of the greatest Christian influencers in the history of the church.

...That around 1516, an Augustinian monk would write,

> *At last, by the mercy of God, meditating day and night, I gave heed to the context of the words, namely, "In it the righteousness of God is revealed, as it is written, 'He who through faith is righteous shall live.'" There I began to understand that the righteousness of God is that by which the righteous lives by a gift of God, namely by faith. And this is the meaning: the righteousness of God is revealed by the gospel, namely, the passive righteousness with which merciful God justifies us by faith, as it is written, "He who through faith is righteous shall live." Here I felt that I was altogether born again and had entered paradise itself through open gates.*

Martin Luther would be converted through his reading of Romans 1:16-17.

...That concerning May 24, 1738 John Wesley wrote,

In the evening I went very unwillingly to a society in Aldersgate Street, where one was reading Luther's preface to the Epistle to the Romans. About a quarter before nine, while he was describing the change which God works in the heart through faith in Christ, I felt my heart strangely warmed. I felt I did trust in Christ, Christ alone, for salvation; and an assurance was given me that he had taken away my sins, even mine, and saved me from the law of sin and death.

Wesley, like Augustine and Luther, was converted through the book of Romans.

...That Robert Moffat, one of the very first missionaries to Africa and David Livingstone's father- in-law, would be converted through reading the eighth chapter of Romans.

...That in 1922 Karl Barth would rock the religious world of his day with his commentary on Romans.

Of course Phoebe had no idea the avalanche God would create through the little pebble He gave her to toss. True, Paul wrote it. But equally true, Phoebe delivered it. Suppose she hadn't quite bothered to be sure it got there? Or she carelessly lost it? Fortunately for us and untold millions of saints she was faithful with her pebble. May God grant that we be equally faithful with ours, no matter how small or insignificant it may seem today. Things like helping in the nursery, teaching second grade Sunday school, setting up chairs before the service, making snacks for the kitchen, reaching out to the homeless stranger, inviting the international student over for dinner, etc. seldom gain much attention in the church world. But these pebbles, tossed in the power of the Spirit for the glory of God, are headline news in heaven. And there is no telling which pebble may go farther than we could ever dream of. Just ask Phoebe. Her pebble is still on the move. And so is yours, my friend. So is yours. God is making sure of it.

FLASHPOINT
Toss the pebble; God will take care of the avalanche.

Influence Beyond Our Time

"Therefore we also, since we are surrounded by so great a cloud of witnesses, let us lay aside every weight, and the sin which so easily ensnares us, and let us run with endurance the race that is set before us," Heb. 12:1

· I take it from this passage that our lives are on display to those who have finished their course before us. They are, as it were, cheering us on. I like the way Eugene Peterson paraphrases this passage in *The Message*—*"Do you see what this means—all these pioneers who blazed the way, all these veterans cheering us on? It means we'd better get on with it."* As we run our race, we do well to remember the stories of those who ran before us. Their legacies. Their examples. We need them for our race. Here's just one example of what I'm talking about:

Pliny was the Roman governor in Asia Minor during the early second century. He was so often confused by what to do with a new sect called "Christians" that he wrote a now famous letter to the Emperor Trajan asking for his advice. A typical situation of what he encountered is the following:

A certain unknown Christian was brought before Pliny. Finding little fault in him, the governor threatened him. "I will banish thee," he said. *"Thou canst not,"* was the reply, *"for all the world is my Father's house."*

"Then I will slay thee," said the Governor.

"Thou canst not," answered the Christian, *"for my life is hid with Christ in God."*

"I will take away thy possessions," continued Pliny.

"Thou canst not, for my treasure is in heaven," replied the believer.

"I will drive thee away from man and thou shalt have no friend left," was the final threat.

And the calm reply once more was, *"Thou canst not, for I have an unseen Friend from Whom thou art not able to separate me."*

Personally, I look forward to meeting that Christian one day. And thanking him for the encouragement and inspiration his encounter with Pliny brought me and countless others over the centuries. My guess is he'll just shake his head and grin modestly. You see, he had no idea how far his godly response to a difficult situation would travel. And neither do you know, my friend, how far your God-enabled response to a difficult situation will travel. Just know that it will (I Cor. 15:58; Phil. 1:6; II Tim.1:12). God makes sure of that.

FLASHPOINT
Godly responses travel farther than we think.

Light

FIRE'S BRILLIANCE

*"I believe in Christianity as I believe that
the sun has risen: not only because I see it,
but because by it I see everything else."*

– C.S. LEWIS –

A mong the more crucial things fire provides is light. It was by the light of the fireplace that young Abraham Lincoln voraciously devoured every book he could get his hands on. It was by the light of a burning lantern that Paul Revere instructed Robert Newman, the sexton of the Old North Church, to send a signal to alert colonists in Charlestown as to the movements of the British troops—"one if by land, two if by sea." And it is by light that we begin and by light that we progress in our Christian walk. "Then Jesus spoke to them again, saying, 'I am the light of the world. He who follows Me shall not walk in darkness, but have the light of life.'" (Jn. 8:12)

These devotions focus on two primary aspects of light. First, light received. In other words, we will look at what it means that "God who commanded light to shine out of darkness,... has shone in our hearts to give the light of the knowledge of the glory of God in the face of Jesus Christ." II Cor. 4:6. Our meditations will be on the stunning, overwhelmingly brilliant realities of who our Savior is and what he has provided for us. Secondly, we will contemplate light reflected. Paul writes, "For you were once darkness, but now you are light in the Lord. Walk as children of light. (for the fruit of the Spirit is in all goodness, righteousness, and truth)," (Eph. 5:8-9.) These reflections will center on what it means to live a life which mightily reflects heaven's light to earth's inhabitants.

The Glory of the Routine

"Whether, therefore, you eat or drink or whatever you do, do all to the glory of God." I Cor. 10:31

This passage forever decimates the possibility of a routine life. Just flat blows it out of the water. That doesn't mean life for the believer isn't daily. Or ordinary. Or tiresomely predictable. But what it does mean is that God has introduced into our lives a high-stepping purpose for going about the seemingly routine. When the ordinary activities and responsibilities of life are carried out with an eye on bringing God's spectacular-ness (His glory) out into the open, we are immediately airlifted out of ordinary, inconsequential living. Martin Luther put it so well when he said, *"The maid who sweeps her kitchen is doing the will of God just as much as the monk who prays—not because she may sing a Christian hymn as she sweeps but because God loves clean floors."* I love that thought.

Nothing is more routine than eating or drinking, which is probably why Paul chose these two activities to highlight. But so is sweeping floors, washing dishes, changing diapers, filling up the car, getting kids to school, filing expense reports, brushing teeth, etc. And not one of these seemingly mundane parts of life is viewed by God as unimportant. Or secular. They are all potential knot holes in the fence of life which provide opportunities for those around to catch at least a small glimpse of the coming world. And if not to those around us in the human realm, then to those above us in the angelic realm, *"for we are made a spectacle unto the world, and to angels, and to men."* (I Cor.4:9)

It is in the daily, seemingly routine aspects of life on this planet that our greatest opportunities for spiritual display are often found. A well-swept floor provides just as much opportunity for the advancement of God's kingdom as a well-preached sermon. And that, friend, is the glory of the routine. And may I say that is one of the things I absolutely love about our faith!

> **FLASHPOINT**
> The glory of God insures that nothing in our life is insignificant.

God Most Unmanageable

"No one is so fierce that he would dare stir him up. Who then is able to stand against Me? Who has preceded Me, that I should pay him? Everything under heaven is Mine."
Job 41:11

It is a dangerous thing to play God. To demand satisfactory answers from the Sovereign of the universe concerning His management style is not for the faint-hearted. It takes tremendous chutzpah to put Yahweh on trial and shouldn't be attempted by just anyone. In fact, it's really best that no one try it. Just ask Job, the most righteous man of his day.

He finally got his day in court (Job 23:1-7; 38:1-41;34). Read the passages and you'll see it didn't go so well for him. Seems he had a hard time coming up with answers when cross-examined about his own omniscience, omnipotence, and omnipresence. And while God delighted in and even boasted about Job's righteousness (Job 1:8; 2:3), He refused to be handcuffed by it. And that, my friend, is an easy trap for all of us to fall into.

God's response to Job's demands that his righteous living be more carefully taken into account was essentially this, as one writer put it:

Job, please tell me whom I am obligated to give answers or blessings to. You are a righteous man, my friend, and I appreciate that very much. But your righteousness does not put Me into debt to you. Everything I have given you and will ever give you is of grace. It is only the arrogant foolishness of your flesh that makes you believe that you can keep Me in check or your life intact (as you define it) through right living. Job, your life will always be lived in the grip of sovereign mystery; don't try to put me into your grip of obligated reward. My dear Job, you can worship Me or you can resent Me; but you cannot manage Me.

Frederick Buechner describes it like this:

God doesn't explain. He explodes. He asks Job who he thinks he is anyway. He says that to try to explain the kind of things Job wants explaining would be like trying to explain Einstein to a little-neck clam...God doesn't reveal his grand design. He reveals Himself.

To his credit, Job allowed himself to be broken over the arrogance of his righteousness. He went from being a godly man to a godlier man. From a good man to a better man. Most of all, he became an even greater worshipper (Job 42:1-6). A more humbled worshipper. A more intimate worshipper. And a deeply satisfied worshipper of an unmanageable God. The only kind of God there is.

> **FLASHPOINT**
> Righteous living delights but does not obligate God.

The Danger of Safeguarded Grace

"What shall we say then? Shall we continue in sin that grace may abound?" Rom. 6:1

Is anyone in our churches *even* asking this question to-day? Are there places where the gospel is preached with such unrestrained exuberance in highlighting God's free offer of salvation through grace and grace alone, that people are wondering if it means they can live however they want after conversion and still go to heaven? Fortunately there are, but they are very few and far between. *We are so afraid that people will abuse grace that we have taken it upon our-selves to erect safeguards to prevent that from ever happening.* But the reality is this: if grace does not have the potential to be abused neither will it have the power to transform. Paul understood that his proclamation *"where sin abounded, grace abounded much more"* (Rom. 5:20) might lead the Romans to believe they were free to sin as much as they liked because grace would cancel out (*"abounded much more"*) any amount of sin in their lives. So he anticipated their question— *"What shall we say then?"* I fear that very, very few people in our day would even have this same question cross their minds in most presentations of the gospel. We are more concerned about keeping people morally respectable than helping them become completely bowled over by the as-tonishing grace of God.

Whenever grace is abused, whenever it is used as a license for sin, it is an awful perversion of the gospel message (Jude 4). This is why Paul answered his own question with the strong words, *"Certainly not! How shall we who died to sin live any longer in it?"* (Rom. 6:2). But it is no less wrong—no less evil—to pull back the reins of grace so that there is no possibility of abuse. For when the reins are drawn back neither is there any possibility for astonishment. Or breath-taking wonder. Or radical life change that is not rule-driven. May the words of one of Britain's finest bible expositors, Dr. Martyn Lloyd-Jones, sink down deeply into our hearts:

> *First of all let me make a comment, to me a very important and vital comment. The true preaching of the gospel of salvation by grace alone always leads to the possibility of this charge being brought against it. There is no better test as to whether a man is really preaching the New Testament gospel of salvation than this, that some people might misunderstand it and misinterpret it to mean that it really amounts to this, that because you are saved by grace alone it does not matter at all what you do; you can go on sinning as much as you like because it will redound all the more to the glory of grace. That is a very good test of gospel preaching. If my preaching and presentation of the gospel of salvation does not expose it to that misunderstanding, then it is not the gospel.*

> *...indeed that was...said about the preaching of Martin Luther. They said, 'This man who was a priest has changed the*

*doctrine in order to justify his own marriage and his own lust',
and so on. 'This man', they said, 'is an antinomian; and that is
heresy.' That is the very charge they brought against him. It was
also brought against George Whitefield two hundred years ago.
It is the charge that formal dead Christianity—if there is such
a thing—has always brought against this startling, staggering
message, that God 'justifies the ungodly'…*

*That is my comment; and it is a very important comment for
preachers. I would say to all preachers: If your preaching of salvation has not been misunderstood in that way, then you had
better examine your sermons again, and you had better make sure
that you really are preaching the salvation that is offered in the
New Testament to the ungodly, to the sinner, to those who are
dead in trespasses and sins, to those who are enemies of God.
There is this kind of dangerous element about the true presentation of the doctrine of salvation.*

All I can say is Amen and Amen. Thank you good doctor, we need these words.

> **FLASHPOINT**
> If grace does not have the potential to be
> abused, it will not have the power to transform.

No Greater Drama

"Who are You, Lord?" Acts 9:5

Theology. It is a tragedy of unspeakable proportions that this word has somehow become associated with a dry, somewhat dull, usually non-applicable perusal of the Person of God. The word literally means *"the doctrine of God"* and if anything was meant to take our breath away, set fire to our hearts, and radically alter the steps of our lives; surely this is it. Doctrine, or "dogma" as it is often referred to, cannot be dull if it is referring to God. Dorothy Sayers writes,

> *We are constantly assured that the churches are empty because preachers insist too much upon doctrine—'dull dogma,' as people call it. The fact is the precise opposite. It is the neglect of dogma that makes for dullness. The Christian faith is the most exciting drama that ever staggered the imagination of man—and the dogma is the drama. . . .*
>
> *So that is the outline of the official story—the tale of the time when God was the under-dog and got beaten, when He submitted to the conditions He had laid down and became a man like the men He had made, and the men He had made broke Him and killed Him. This is the dogma we find so dull—this terrifying drama of which God is the victim and hero. If this is dull, then what, in Heaven's name, is worthy to be called exciting?*

Amen and amen!

A.W. Tozer puts it so well in his classic work, "The Knowledge of the Holy":

> *If some watcher or holy one who has spent his glad centuries by the sea of fire were to come to earth, how meaningless to him would be the ceaseless chatter of the busy tribes of men. How strange to him and how empty would sound the flat, stale, and profitless words heard in the average pulpit from week to week. And were such a one to speak on earth would he not speak of God? Would he not charm and fascinate his hearers with rapturous descriptions of the Godhead? And after hearing him could we ever again consent to listen to anything less than theology, the doctrine of God? Would we not thereafter demand of those who would presume to teach us that they speak to us from the mount of divine vision or remain silent altogether?*

How I love his statement, *"And were such a one to speak on earth would he not speak of God? Would he not charm and fascinate his hearers with rapturous descriptions of the Godhead?"* What could possibly be more endlessly fascinating, unimaginably heart ravishing, or thoroughly life transforming than an all-out assault to answer the question which dominated the whole of Paul's life—*"Who are You, Lord ?"*

It was his white hot pursuit to personally and intimately answer this question that became the preeminent pursuit of his life. *"That I may know Him..."* (Phil. 3:10-15). It was the answer to this question that sustained him in his last hours. *"...nevertheless I am not ashamed, for I know Whom I have believed..."* (II Tim. 1:12). And I seriously doubt you could convince Paul that theology was dry, dull, or seemingly impractical. Easier to convince an adolescent male that sex is boring or a young maiden that she will yawn at her wedding. No, theology properly pursued, is the greatest adventure entrusted to man. May God grant that none of us settle for anything less.

> **FLASHPOINT**
> True Christian doctrine brings fire to the heart as well as light to the mind.

The Value of Problem Passages

"But Samuel said, "As your sword has made women childless, so shall your mother be childless among women." And Samuel hacked Agag in pieces before the LORD in Gilgal." I Sam. 15:33

Seems like overkill (no pun intended) doesn't it? After all, why couldn't the passage just say, *"Samuel killed Agag"*? In fact, the NIV tamely translates it that very way, *"And Samuel put Agag to death before the LORD at Gilgal."* Certainly this is a much less graphic way of describing Agag's execution. Gentler, easier to read.

But that's not what the Hebrew text reads! It most literally reads, *"Samuel hacked Agag in pieces."* No way around it. Is there really a need for the additional gory details? And then it even adds a worship component with the phrase, *"before the Lord."* What on earth is going on here? How do we deal with such a seemingly un-Christian passage of scripture?

What we *don't* do is ignore it. Minimize it. Run from it. Put it back where it came from and make sure to skip over it next time we're reading I Samuel. It is precisely passages like this that show us how much more room there is to go in our quest of knowing God. Of knowing God *as He is,* and not as we have assumed Him to be or would like for Him to be. C.S. Lewis has such a great thought on this,

> *If our religion is something objective, then we must never avert our eyes from those elements in it which seem puzzling or repellent; for it will be precisely the puzzling or the repellent which conceals what we do not yet know and need to know.*

Don't pass over his words too quickly; they're too important. If the bible doesn't bother you, it's because you've never read it! Are there passages in the bible you find *"puzzling"*? If not, you're not reading your bible. Are there passages you find actually *"repellent"*? If not, I say again that you are not reading your bible. But, as Lewis says, *"we must not avert our eyes"* from them, for they scream out to us that there is more of God for us to know. To enjoy. To worship. To tremble before. To dance over. Most of all, to be changed by.

We call these verses "problem passages." Fact is, they are no problems to God at all. And they are more than problems to us. They are invitations. Invitations from an unspeakably holy and fiercely loving God to come dine with Him at His table and get to know Him better. And invitations such as that should not be turned down.

> **FLASHPOINT**
> "Problem passages" are our friends, inviting us to know God in ways we have not yet experienced or understood.

The Witness of Work

"Do you see a man who excels in his work? He will stand before kings; He will not stand before unknown men." Pr. 22:29

It matters that we do our work well for many reasons. But one reason according to this passage (one which is often overlooked) is the unique sphere of influence it may well allow us to have. *"...He will stand before kings; He will not stand before unknown men."* Let me illustrate.

James Simpson was born in Scotland on June 7, 1811. At 18 he passed his examination to become a doctor but because he was too young, he had to wait two years to receive his license to practice. At the age of 28 he was appointed to the Chair of Medicine and Midwifery at the University of Edinburgh. He improved the design of obstetric forceps and fought against the contagion of puerperal sepsis. But his most important contribution by far was the development of Chloroform, which absolutely revolutionized anesthesiology. On the day of Simpson's funeral, a Scottish holiday was declared, including the banks and stock markets, with over 100,000 citizens lining the funeral route to the cemetery, while over 1,700 colleagues and business leaders took part in the procession itself.

According to Dr. Simpson though, the greatest discovery of his life was not Chloroform. Toward the end of his life, he was lecturing at the University of Edinburgh. One of the students asked him what he considered his most valuable discovery. A perfect setup! Everyone expected him to recount how he discovered the medical use of chloroform. Instead Dr. Simpson replied, *"My most valuable discovery was when I discovered myself a sinner and that Jesus Christ was my Savior."* The room went silent, needless to say.

A job well done. And through it, a Savior well spotlighted. What an awesome combination! May God grant that we can follow in those same footsteps.

The Power of the Cross

"For I determined not to know anything among you except Jesus Christ and Him crucified." I Cor. 2:2

There is extraordinary, extraordinary power in the cross. This is why Paul refused to succumb to the temptation to win the Corinthians through the means we might have most expected—*"excellence of speech or wisdom...persuasive words of human wisdom"* (I Cor. 2:1, 4). Paul understood one of the most important truths of gospel presentation there is: wisdom may win an argument, but only blood-stained love wins a heart.

David Brainerd, an early American missionary to the native Americans discovered the great reality of the transforming power of the gospel in his ministry. Read carefully his account:

I never got away from Jesus and Him crucified. When my people were gripped by this great evangelical doctrine of Christ and Him crucified, I had no need to give them instructions about morality…I find that my Indians begin to put on the garments of holiness and their common life begins to be sanctified even in small matters when they are possessed by the doctrine of Christ and Him crucified.

Satan wants us to stay away from the cross at all costs. I don't think he really cares what does it, just as long as we don't think about the cross, meditate upon the cross, or become awestruck by the cross. And above all, not proclaim the cross. For at the cross, his cause is placed in its greatest possible jeopardy. At the cross the white hot heat of God's unrelenting love melts the coldness of our hearts and settles forever the question of how much God really loves us. The famed missionary to the Muslims, Samuel Zwemer, put it so well:

The missionary among Moslems (to whom the Cross of Christ is a stumbling-block and the atonement foolishness) is driven daily to deeper meditation on the mystery of redemption, and to a stronger conviction that here is the very heart of our message and our mission…

If the Cross of Christ is anything to the mind, it is surely everything—the most profound reality and the sublimest mystery. One comes to realize that literally all the wealth and glory of the gospel centres here. The Cross is the pivot as well as the centre of

New Testament thought. It is the exclusive mark of the Christian faith, the symbol of Christianity and its cynosure.

… We rediscover the apostolic emphasis on the Cross when we read the gospel with Moslems. We find that although the offence of the Cross remains, its magnetic power is irresistible.

I love his phrase, *"its magnetic power is irresistible."* In the midst of a church culture that focuses upon so many good things—strong families, good finances, healthy relationships, spiritual disciplines, etc.— we are in grave, grave danger of focusing upon everything but what matters most. I have no doubt whatsoever that if Paul were given opportunity to speak to the 21st century church, one of his very first admonitions would be this—*"Make much of the cross, make much of the cross, make much of the cross!"* It was what Paul lived for and what he died for. And what he saw change lives like nothing else. May God grant that we follow in his steps.

FLASHPOINT
Make much of the blood. Go often to the cross.

Kindness and Severity

"Behold then the kindness and severity of God," Rom. 11:22

J.I. Packer, in his classic work *Knowing God*, noted that the most important word in this verse is the word *"and."* How easily we focus on one side or the other, but the true and living God exists at both ends of the spectrum and everywhere in between. God is not only unspeakably kind but also unimaginably severe. He is not only a God of flaming vengeance, but One of breathtaking mercy. One of the clearest evidences of this is the only two places mankind will spend eternity: *heaven* or *hell*. God's kindness to the infinite degree or God's wrath to the infinite degree.

Jonathan Edwards is probably best known for his sermon, "Sinners in the Hands of an Angry God." He preached the sermon out of compassion for his people, wanting them to realize what was at stake if they callously spurned God's offer of salvation through the blood of His only Son. In it he writes concerning hell:

It would be dreadful to suffer this fierceness and wrath of Almighty God one moment; but you must suffer it to all eternity. There will be no end to this exquisite horrible misery. When you look forward, you shall see a long for ever, a boundless duration before you, which will swallow up your thoughts, and amaze your soul; and you will absolutely despair of ever having any deliverance, any end, any mitigation, any rest at all. You will know certainly that you must wear out long ages, millions of millions of ages, in wrestling and conflicting with this almighty merciless vengeance; and then when you have so done, when so many ages have actually been spent by you in this manner, you will know that all is but a point to what remains. So that your punishment will indeed be infinite.

But Edwards preached monumentally more on God's love than his wrath.

He could just have easily written concerning heaven:

It would be wonderful to enjoy this grace and kindness of Almighty God one moment; but you will enjoy it to all eternity. There will be no end to this exquisite joy. When you look forward, you shall see a long for ever, a boundless duration before you, which will swallow up your thoughts, and amaze your soul; and you will absolutely rejoice in not having any deliverance, any end, any mitigation, any rest at all. You will know certainly that you must wear out long ages, millions of millions of ages, in worship and adoration of this almighty consuming kindness; and then when you have so done, when so many ages have actually been spent by you in this manner, you will know that all is but a point to what remains. So that your joy will indeed be infinite.

God is not somewhat kind and somewhat severe. He is kind beyond all possible description and severe beyond all possible imagination. Our trembling yet bold approach to the Father, our reverent and deep enjoyment of the Son, and our sacred and joyous fellowship with the Spirit all require one very critical component—that we keep the *"and"* firmly in place.

> **FLASHPOINT**
> "Behold the kindness *and* severity of the Lord."

Heat

FIRE'S WARMTH

*"Ye angels of God, who behold his face, explain
to me the sacred mystery; tell me how this heavenly
flame began; unriddle its wondrous generation.
Who hath animated this mortal flame with celestial fire,
and given a clod of earth this divine ambition?
What could kindle it but the breath of God,
which kindled up my soul…"*

– Elizabeth Rowe –

Fire disperses more than light. It provides heat as well. Simply put, there is no such thing as fire which is light-free or warmth-free. And so it is with true spirituality. A vital, healthy, deepening relationship with Christ not only provides the light of God's truth but also the warmth of God's Spirit. In other words, propositional truth and personal experience are not at odds with each other. They are, in fact, the very best of friends. Jonathan Edwards penned an entire book defending this proposition entitled "Religious Affections." In it he writes,

As there is no true religion where there is nothing else but affection, so there is no true religion where there is no religious affection. As on the one hand, there must be light in the understanding, as well as an affected fervent heart; where there is heat without light, there can be nothing divine or heavenly in that heart; so on the other hand, where there is a kind of light without heat, a head stored with notions and speculations, with a cold and unaffected heart, there can be nothing divine in that light, that knowledge is no true spiritual knowledge of divine things. If the great things of religion are rightly understood, they will affect the heart.

These meditations are devoted to exploring the great reality that "God is Spirit, and those who worship Him must worship in spirit and truth" (Jn. 4:24). What God has joined together let no man put asunder.

Christian Mysticism

"...that He would grant to you...to be strengthened with might through His Spirit in the inner man." Eph.3:16

It is one thing to know about the triune God. It is a very different thing to have one's heart ravished by an experiential encounter with the three Members of the Godhead. Yet this is exactly what Paul prays for in his letter to the Ephesians. In Eph.1:4-14, Paul describes the work of the Trinity in our salvation. He tells us what God the Father has done (Eph.1:4-6), what God the Son has done (Eph.1:7-12), and what God the Holy Spirit has done (Eph.1:13-14). All of this is true for every believer, whether or not it feels real.

But at the end of Ephesians 3, he asks God to make the Trinity an unmistakable, heart-felt, experiential reality to these believers. *"that He* (God the Father) *would grant to you... to be strengthened with might through His Spirit* (God the Holy Spirit) *in the inner man, that Christ* (God the Son) *may dwell* (lit. 'be at home') *in your hearts through faith; that you, being rooted and grounded in love, may be able to comprehend with all the saints what is the width and length and depth and height—to know the love of Christ which passes knowledge; that you may be filled with all the fullness of God"*(Eph.3:14-19). There is an undeniable mysticism to true spirituality. It is what Francis Schaeffer calls *"Christian mysticism."* In *True Spirtuality* he writes:

> *Here is true Christian mysticism. Christian mysticism is not the same as non-Christian mysticism, but I would insist it is not a*

lesser mysticism. Indeed, eventually it is a deeper mysticism, for it is not based on contentless experience, but on historic, space-time reality—on propositional truth. One is not asked to deny the reason, the intellect, in true Christian mysticism...Christian mysticism is communion with Christ. It is Christ bringing forth fruit through me, the Christian.

Yet this is nothing new. Augustine speaks of the same thing in slightly different words as he describes encountering God:

And what do I love when I love You? Not physical beauty...or the radiance of light that pleases the eye, or the sweet melody of old familiar songs, or the fragrance of flowers and ointments and spices... None of these do I love when I love my God.

Yet there is a kind of light, and a kind of melody, and a kind of fragrance, and a kind of food, and a kind of embracing when I love my God. They are the kind of light and sound and odor and food and love that affect the senses of the inner man.

...It hears melodies that never fade with time. It inhales lovely scents that are not blown away by the wind. It eats without diminishing or consuming the supply. It never gets separated from the embrace of God and never gets tired of it. That is what I love when I love my God.

A mind drenched with God's truth and a heart ravished by God's presence are the twin pillars of genuine Godliness. *Always have been...always will be.*

> **FLASHPOINT**
> Truth *and* experience are inseparable friends in vital Christianity.

Our Greatest Treasure

"So Satan answered the Lord and said, 'Does Job fear God for nothing?'" Job 1:9

Satan doesn't believe that anyone serves God because of the sheer joy of relationship. Or that anyone seeks to please God for any other reason than buying Him off. If God didn't provide the earthly benefits, then man would never provide the earthly obedience. And he believes all that for a very simple reason. No one serves him because of relationship. Period.

Nobody goes into Satanism because of love for Satan. They go into it for power, drugs, sex, protection, etc. Because he provides such appealing goods, they are willing to become his worshippers to insure the goods delivery. And the devil cannot believe that men would treat God any other way. Which is where he is wrong. Oh so wrong.

God wins our affections, gains our worship, and garnishes our praise through something far more powerful than earthly goods. He bowls us over by Who He is. Pure and simple. Breathtaking holiness, astonishing grace, incomparable love, and a host of other white-hot attributes compel us to pursue God simply for the unrivaled treasure and pleasure of relationship. The Puritan Thomas Goodwin wrote, *"I have known men who came to God for nothing else but to come to Him, they so loved Him. They scorned to soil Him or themselves with any other errand than just purely to be alone with Him in His presence."*

I love his statement, *"They scorned to soil Him or themselves with any other errand than just purely to be alone with Him in His presence."* This is something completely incomprehensible to Satan. But wonderful beyond all description to God's children. And one of our great privileges before the seen and unseen world is to scream by our lives that God is worthy of our obedience and affection even if the only thing we get on this planet is Him. As if that wasn't more than enough. And this is where Satan was so very wrong in his evaluation of Job. *"So Satan answered the Lord and said, 'Does Job fear God for nothing?'"* He assumed that if Job didn't get earthly benefits, he was getting *"nothing."* But what he missed was that without any earthly possessions or treasures, Job was still unimaginably wealthy. He had God. And so do we. As A.W. Tozer writes in his classic work *The Pursuit of God:*

> *The man who has God for his treasure has all things in One. Many ordinary treasures may be denied him, or if he is allowed*

to have them, the enjoyment of them will be so tempered that they will never be necessary to his happiness. Or if he must see them go, one after one, he will scarcely feel a sense of loss, for having the Source of all things he has in One all satisfaction, all pleasure, all delight. Whatever he may lose he has actually lost nothing, for he now has it all in One, and he has it purely, legitimately and forever.

Let Satan scorn all that he wants. Let him take away all that God allows. What he can never touch or understand is our greatest treasure—vital intimacy with a God Who reaches places in the human heart which earthly treasures never can.

FLASHPOINT
Being reduced to having only God is life's greatest treasure.

KINDLING FOR THE FIRE

First Call

**"Then He appointed twelve, that they might be with Him
and that He might send them out to preach."** Mk. 3:14

God's first calling on our lives is not *usefulness*. It is *intimacy*. Like the first disciples, Christ's premier purpose for
our lives is for us to be *"with Him."* Secondarily, very secondarily, He then sends us *"out to"* minister. How easily we lose
sight of this! And when He does not seem to be sending us
out, when no doors of ministry opportunity seem open, we
so quickly fret that God appears to have put us on the shelf.
As usual, Oswald Chambers has a great word concerning
this: *"Has God put you on the shelf deliberately? Why cannot He
be glorified by a man in the dust as well as in the sunshine? We are
not here to tell God what to do with us, but to let Him use us as He
chooses. Remember, God's main concern is that we are more interested
in Him than in work for Him. Once you are rooted and grounded in
Christ the greatest thing you can do is to be. Don't try and be useful;
be yourself and God will use you to further His ends."*

What a great, great word for all of us. I am particularly
struck by his statement, *"Remember, God's main concern is that
we are more interested in Him than in work for Him."* That was
exactly the problem for the church of Ephesus—they were
more interested in work for Him than Him.

> *I know your works, your labor, your patience, and that you can-
> not bear those who are evil. And you have tested those who say
> they are apostles and are not, and have found them liars; and*

*you have persevered and have patience, and have labored for My name's sake and have not become weary. Nevertheless I have this against you, that you have left your first love... (*Rev. 2:1-8)

That was exactly the issue for Martha. She was more interested in work for Him than Him. *"But Martha was distracted with much serving, and she approached Him and said, 'Lord, do You not care that my sister has left me to serve alone? Therefore tell her to help me.' And Jesus answered and said to her, 'Martha, Martha, you are worried and troubled about many things. But one thing is needed, and Mary has chosen that good part, which will not be taken away from her.'" (*Lk. 10:38-42)

And all, all too often that is exactly our problem as well. Sooner or later, every servant of God must make the determined choice that nothing but nothing matters more in life than spending quiet, extended, unhurried time alone with God. This is not all there is to our spiritual lives, but it is unquestionably our first call and highest privilege. *"Then He appointed twelve, that they might be with Him"* was true not only for the twelve but also us. The depth of our roots matters supremely more than the amount of our fruit. Also, I love his thought, *"Once you are rooted and grounded in Christ the greatest thing you can do is to be. Don't try and be useful; be yourself and God will use you to further His ends."* Amen. The most useful thing many of us can do for God is to quit focusing on our usefulness and reacquaint ourselves with the astonishment and wonder of a first-hand love affair with our Savior. And then just *be.* Just allow the supernatural fruit of abiding in Christ to break forth in unrestrained fullness.

For in reality, Christ-soaked *being* is the most powerful *doing* we have going for us this side of eternity.

> **FLASHPOINT**
> The depth of our roots matters supremely
> more than the amount of our fruit.

Happiness, Pleasure, or Joy?

"Whom having not seen you love. Though now you do not see Him, yet believing, you rejoice with joy inexpressible and full of glory," I Pet 1:8

"Joy inexpressible." Hmm, I wonder how often I've actually tasted that commodity. C.S. Lewis makes an important distinction in separating joy from happiness or pleasure. *"Happiness"* is the presence of favorable external circumstances. This word, in fact, gives itself away by its etymology. It comes from the Latin root *"hap"* which means "chance." This is why *perhaps* and *perchance* mean the same thing. Happiness is wholly based on chance. The chance possibility that there is enough money in the bank

(is there ever enough?). The chance possibility that one's accomplishments are appropriately recognized and honored. The chance possibility that we get the new car, the new home, the better job, etc. There is nothing wrong with happiness; it is one of the blessings of God upon this earth. But it ought not be confused with joy.

"Pleasure" comes as a result of having a bodily appetite fulfilled. A great dinner, a fresh cup of coffee, passionate lovemaking, etc. All of these are wonderful gifts within the appropriate bounds set by God. But they ought not be confused with joy. In this regard Lewis writes, *"Joy is not a substitute for sex; sex is very often a substitute for joy. I sometimes wonder whether all pleasures are not substitutes for joy."*

Joy is in a league all of its own. First of all, it is completely independent of external circumstances. In fact, it sometimes flourishes where external circumstances are the worst. As a third-century man was anticipating death, he penned these last words to a friend:

> *It's a bad world, an incredibly bad world. But I have discovered in the midst of it a quiet and holy people who have learned a great secret. They have found a joy which is a thousand times better than any pleasure of our sinful life. They are despised and persecuted, but they care not. They are masters of their souls. They have overcome the world. These people are the Christians— and I am one of them.*

The recipients of this epistle from Peter were undergoing a severe *"fiery trial,"* yet their joy was *"inexpressible"*

(I Pet.1:6; 4:12). Paul wrote to the persecuted Thessalonian believers, *"And you became followers of us and of the Lord, having received the word in much affliction, with joy of the Holy Spirit"* (I Thess. 1:6).

Joy is also deeper and purer than happiness or pleasure. *"You will show me the path of life; in Your presence is fullness of joy; at Your right hand are pleasures forevermore."* (Ps. 16:11). Joy reaches into depths of the human spirit where happiness and pleasure simply can't go. Kirby Page writes, *"The word 'joy' is too great and grand to be confused with the superficial things we call 'happiness'. It was joy and peace that Jesus left men in His will."* Another writes, *"Joy is the echo of God's life within."*

Joy is more fickle than happiness or pleasure. We can't control it quite the way we can happiness or pleasure. Frederick Buechner writes, *"Happiness turns up more or less where you would expect it. Joy, on the other hand, is notoriously unpredictable as is the One who gives it."* Amen. Joy is not something we find; it is something that finds us. Sometimes at the most unpredictable times. But it has the best chance of finding us when we are preoccupied not with joy but with the Joy-giver, when our great pursuit is not for a certain experience but for a certain Person. His name is Jesus, the only One Who has ever said, *"These things I have spoken to you, that My joy may remain in you, and that your joy may be full."* (Jn. 15:10-11). May God grant that our joy-tasting increases as our Christ-abiding deepens.

FLASHPOINT
Joy is the by-product of a greater pursuit than joy.

Christian Buddhism

"Open your mouth wide, and I will fill it." Ps.81:10

I love our Lord's invitation here—*"Open your mouth wide..."* He isn't calling us to restrain our longings, keep a stiff upper lip, and simply be content with the meager portions we have accumulated. No, a thousand times no! He is inviting us to stretch open our mouths as wide as we possibly can and take in all that He longs to provide. *"...and I will fill it".* We can't open our mouths widely enough that He runs out of supply to fill them. For His supply and our feast are exactly the same—God Himself. Our Lord takes no delight in drab, dour denial of self under the guise of "contentment." He delights in seeing his children passionate enough and trusting enough to come hard after Him for all they can taste of Trinitarian cuisine.

Much of what is called "contentment" among Christians is really little more than sanctified Buddhism. The goal of Buddhism is *nirvana*, the state of tranquility and contentment that comes from having one's desires extinguished. One is satisfied not because longings have been met, but because they have been annihilated. Far too many of us (myself very much included) find it easier to pretend that we don't really care that much than to risk opening our mouths wide and potentially finding ourselves disappointed. As usual, C.S. Lewis puts it so well in *The Weight of Glory:*

> *If there lurks in most modern minds the notion that to desire our own good and earnestly to hope for the enjoyment of it is a bad thing, I submit that this notion has crept in from Kant and the Stoics and is no part of the Christian faith. Indeed, if we consider the unblushing promises of reward and the staggering nature of the rewards promised in the Gospels, it would seem our Lord finds our desires not too strong, but too weak. We are half-hearted creatures, fooling about with drink and sex and ambition when infinite joy is offered us, like an ignorant child who wants to go on making mud pies in a slum because he cannot imagine what is meant by the offer of a holiday at the sea. We are far too easily pleased."*

So, so true. I love his last statement, *"We are far too easily pleased."* True contentment is not pretending the raging thirst within us is a ghost; it's taking our real thirst with all its passionate neediness and diving headlong into the river of God to drink. It's taking the risk to open our mouths wide as they will go and trusting that the Architect of our longings will also be the Supplier of them. Both in eternity...and now.

FLASHPOINT
God cannot give His best to close-mouthed saints. Open wide!

Extreme Worship – At Both Ends

"One thing I have desired of the Lord, that will I seek: that I may dwell in the house of the Lord all the days of my life, to behold the beauty of the Lord, and to inquire in His temple." Ps.27:4

I'm struck by the wonderful symmetry found here in David's pursuit of God. He came as both a passionate worshipper (*"to behold the beauty of the Lord"*) and an eager learner (*"to inquire in His temple"*). He desired to be ravished by the sight of God's stunning beauty and blazing perfection.

He also longed to know more and more fully the ways and wisdom of His Lord. He was an all-out extremist—but an extremist at both ends of the spectrum. What an important combination! How desperately it is needed today.

All too often our churches and individual Christians are focusing on one of these to the neglect of the other. For some, it is preoccupation with passion for God through worship (which is seen primarily as music), and what matters most is that the heart has been touched and stirred by its encounter. Others are equally absorbed with sound bible doctrine, and what matters most to them is that their minds have been stimulated to consider the word of God in new and fresh ways. Both have their crucial roles in true spirituality, and one can never go too deeply into either. But the burning heart and the enlightened mind must always walk arm in arm, as necessary complements to each other. Bishop Moule, a great scholar himself, put it so well when he wrote:

> *Beware of an untheological devotion. There is no contradiction between mind and heart, between theology and devotion. Devotional hours do not mean hours when thought is absent; on the contrary, if devotion is to be real it should be characterized by thought. Meditation is not abstraction, nor is devotion dreaminess. 'Thou shalt love the Lord thy God with all thy...mind' is an essential part of 'the first and great commandment' (Matt. 22:37-38). A piety that is mere pietism, evangelicalism that does not continually ponder the profound truths of the New Testament, can never be strong or do any true service to the gospel*

cause. We must indeed beware of 'untheological devotion.'

But we must also beware of 'undevotional theology'. This is the opposite error, and it constitutes an equally grave danger. A hard, dry, intellectual study of theology will yield no spiritual fruit... it is the heart that makes the theologian; and a theology that does not spring from spiritual experience is doomed to decay, to deadness, and to disaster.

How profoundly insightful! And how profoundly important for healthy and thriving spirituality.

> **FLASHPOINT**
> Doctrine and Devotion are best of friends.

Filling in the Blank

"For to me, to live is Christ, and to die is gain." Phil.1:21

For me to live is _____. How would you fill in the blank? We all fill it in with something. Prestige, money, alcohol, sex, sports, a lover, family, job, ministry, etc. are but a few of the myriad of possibilities. We all fill in the blank with something. But our lives will never be what they were created to be or redeemed to be until the blank is filled in with a *someone*, rather than a *something*. The right Someone, of course.

The following is a letter which a communist worker in Mexico wrote to his fiancée in breaking off their engagement many years ago. In part it reads,

We Communists have a high casualty rate...We've been described as fanatics. We are fanatics. Our lives are dominated by one great overshadowing factor: the struggle for world Communism.

We Communists have a philosophy of life which no amount of money could buy. We have a cause to fight for, a definite purpose in life. We subordinate our petty personal selves into a great movement of humanity, and if our personal lives seem hard, or our egos appear to suffer through subordination to the party, then we are adequately compensated by the thought that each of us in his small way is contributing to something new and true and better for mankind.

There is one thing in which I am dead earnest and that is the Communist cause. It is my life, my business, my religion, my hobby, my sweetheart, my wife and mistress, my bread and meat. I work at it in the daytime and dream of it at night. Its hold on me grows, not lessens as time goes on. Therefore I cannot carry on a friendship, a love affair, or even a conversation without relat-

ing to this force which both drives and guides my life. I evaluate people, books, ideas and actions according to how they affect the Communist cause and by their attitude toward it.

This man's blank was filled in with a cause, one that seemed so intoxicating and significant at the time. Yet time has turned his dreams into dust and his efforts and sacrifices into ashes. This is inevitably what happens when our blank is filled with a something. Paul chose to spend his few days on earth filling in his blank with a Someone. A perfect Someone. A Someone named Jesus. And truly, the world has never been the same. He could have just as easily have written:

There is one Person in Whom I am in dead earnest and that is Jesus Christ. He is my life, my business, my religion, my hobby, my sweetheart, my wife and mistress, my bread and meat. I work with Him in the daytime and dream of Him at night. His hold on me grows, not lessens as time goes on. Therefore I cannot carry on a friendship, a love affair, or even a conversation without relating it to this Person who both drives and guides my life. I evaluate people, books, ideas and actions according to how they glorify Christ and by their attitude toward Him.

God bless you my friend as you go about filling in your blank today. And may God grant to all of us, that in ever increasing measure, our blank is filled in with a Someone. *The Someone.* The only Someone Who can fully fill in our blank.

> **FLASHPOINT**
> May our blank be always filled with a
> Someone. The Someone.

Shadows
FIRE'S FLICKERING

"I have had great experience of God's hearing my Prayers, and returning comfortable Answers to me, either in granting the Thing I prayed for, or else in satissfying my mind without it; and I have been confident it hath been from him, because I have found my heart through his goodnes enlarged in Thankfulnes to him.

I have often been perplexed that I have not found that constant Joy in my Pilgrimage and refreshing which I supposed most of the servants of God have; although he hath not left me altogether without the wittnes of his holy spirit... Yet have I many Times sinkings and droopings, and not enjoyed that felicity that somtimes I have done."

— ANNE BRADSTREET —

R arely does a fire burn without a shadow being present. A shadow occurs when there is not enough light to completely obliterate all darkness and there is not enough darkness to completely obscure all light. In a sense, every shadow represents the struggle between light and darkness to overpower one another. Just like the Christian life.

True spirituality is messy. Just no way around it. It is the combination of spiritual highs and spiritual lows, the co-mingling of God's Spirit and our flesh, the walking hand in hand of faith and doubt, and the never ending battle to overcome lust, greed, and arrogance. It is waking up one day sensing the immediate, strong presence of the Lord and waking up the very next day wondering if He even exists. It's being unspeakably grateful to God in the morning and spitting mad at Him (if we'll admit it) by noon. Who of us can't relate to the words "...Lord, I believe; help my unbelief!"? (Mk. 9:24)

Nobody is fast forwarded to spiritual maturity on this planet. Spirituality therefore is a journey, not a state. A journey that inevitably includes flickering faith and struggling spirituality. But struggle is always a good sign. It shows there is life. These devotions are devoted to encourage you, my fellow struggler, to keep pressing on until spirituality does become a state and our warfare on this planet is permanently ended.

Honest Spirituality

"And at the ninth hour Jesus cried out with a loud voice, saying, 'Eloi, Eloi, lama sabachthani?' which is translated, 'My God, My God, why have You forsaken Me?'" Mark 15:34

Teresa De Avila, the great mystic saint of the middle ages, is reported to have once cried out to heaven, *"God, no wonder You have so few friends, look how You treat them!"* Personally I find that kind of spiritual honesty very refreshing as well as encouraging.

We do a grave disservice to the people around us if we hide the fact that at times we struggle with God. Sometimes, very intensely. If we're living in the same fallen world everyone else is, then there will be times in all of our lives that the words that best describe our relationship with God are: Abandoned...Confused...Hurt...Second Guessing The Whole Thing...Depressed...Angry...Bone Weary...Ready To Throw In The Towel...etc. Sometimes those feelings are the result of sin in our lives. More often than I think we realize, they are simply clear evidences of our humanity. Just like our Lord.

I'm totally intrigued with this passage. At one level, this is terrible marketing on the part of our Lord. He has just spent the last three and a half years telling people how close He and the Father are. So close in fact, that they are one. (Jn.10:30). Now, at the very end, one would think He would keep His doubts under close wrap. At most, He might whis-

per His feelings of betrayal. But what does the text say? "…
Jesus cried out with a loud voice…". Eugene Peterson renders
it well, *"Jesus groaned out of the depths, crying loudly"* (The Message). Careful Jesus, someone might hear You!

But maybe Jesus wanted people to hear. Maybe He
wanted us to know that struggle is part and parcel of walking closely with God. Was His cry the result of sin? Clearly,
unquestionably not. It was the passionate expression of
unbridled humanity. He is doing far more than simply
quoting Ps. 22:1 on the cross. He is giving full vent to the
excruciating reality of being separated from the Father's
presence for the first and only time in all eternity. An agony you and I cannot even begin to imagine. But an agony
that He was unwilling to repress, unwilling to pretend
didn't exist.

And I, for one, am so glad that He didn't. It reminds
me that there is nothing spiritual about stiff arming our
humanity and pretending that we don't hurt as badly as
we hurt or aren't confused as badly as we are confused.
And it reminds me that honest admission of our struggles
with faith does not put unbelievers off. In fact, you'll note
that just four verses later the Roman Centurion declares,
"Truly this Man was the Son of God!" (Mk. 15:38). Honest,
ruthlessly honest spirituality is the need of the hour. Always has been, always will be. God bless you, my fellow
struggler.

> **FLASHPOINT**
> Honest admission of spiritual struggle has tremendous drawing power.

Conflicted Faith

"Immediately the father of the child cried out and said with tears, "Lord, I believe; help my unbelief!" Mark 9:24

I love this scripture. If I had to pick a life verse, this would probably be it. How often I find my faith to be just like this father's—conflicted, wavering, up and down. I take tremendous encouragement in the fact that Jesus graciously responded to this father's imperfect, fragmented, conflicted faith and healed his son. Maybe conflicted faith is not loss of faith. Maybe it's simply part and parcel of walking authentically with God on this sin-riddled planet. One believer wrote with raw honesty concerning his grief after his beloved wife died of cancer,

Meanwhile, where is God? This is one of the most disquieting symptoms [of grief]. When you are happy, so happy that you have

no sense of needing Him, so happy that you are tempted to feel His claims upon you as an interruption, if you remember yourself and turn to Him with gratitude and praise, you will be—or so it feels—welcomed with open arms. But go to Him when your need is desperate, when all other help is vain, and what do you find? A door slammed in your face, and a sound of bolting and double bolting on the inside. After that, silence. You may as well turn away. The longer you wait, the more emphatic the silence will become. There are no lights in the windows. It might be an empty house. Was it ever inhabited? It seemed so once, and that seeming was as strong as this. What can this mean? Why is He so present a commander in our time of prosperity and so very absent a help in time of trouble?

Talk to me about the truth of religion and I'll listen gladly. Talk to me about the duty of religion and I'll listen submissively. But don't come talking to me about the consolations of religion or I shall suspect that you don't understand.

Not that I am (I think) in much danger of ceasing to believe in God. The real danger is of coming to believe such dreadful things about Him. The conclusion I dread is not 'So there's no God after all,' but 'So this is what God's really like. Deceive yourself no longer.'

Of course it's easy enough to say that God seems absent at our greatest need because He is absent—non-existent. But then why does He seem so present when, to put it frankly, we don't ask for Him?

This man? C.S. Lewis. That's right, *the* C.S. Lewis— one of the most influential Christian writers in the history of the church. The one who also wrote, *"Joy is the serious business of heaven."* Was Lewis's faith conflicted? Was belief sometimes, if not often, a struggle for him? Did he find himself, like the father in today's passage, partly in and partly out when it came to risking all at faith's table? Absolutely. Of course his faith was conflicted. Of course he struggled. Of course he doubted at times. *Just like all of us.* But he also discovered that faltering faith is not fatal and that God still resides mightily behind the bolted door even when He seems most absent. Even for struggling believers. Especially for struggling believers.

> **FLASHPOINT**
> Nobody is fast-forwarded to maturity.
> Faltering, conflicted faith is a normal part of
> the journey.

Spiritual Schizophrenia

"He burns half of it in the fire; with this half he eats meat... he even warms himself...and the rest of it he makes into a god, his carved image. He falls down before it and worships it; prays to it and says, 'Deliver me, for you are my God." Is.44:16-17

Man is a strange creature indeed. First of all, we are the only beings on the face of the earth who worship. No other creature has a God-ward inclination or any propensity for prayer. We are also the only creatures who manufacture our own gods. And then bow down to the very god we created and ask it to deliver us. Go figure.

Someone once quipped, *"In the beginning God created man, and man has been returning the favor ever since."* I like that. In reality that is exactly what idolatry is—reverse creationism. Man making God in his image according to his likeness. It is also what I like to refer to it as "spiritual schizophrenia." Probably nowhere is that seen more vividly than (Is.44:9-20), a tremendous parody on the whole enterprise of idol manufacturing.

Bottom line is this: We are born into this world with unmanageable needs. In other words we yearn for love, significance, safety, respect, etc. in profoundly intense ways. These needs are so powerful that we can't wish them away, pretend them away, numb them away, or deny them away. So we turn to God to meet these needs. Or a god. But we want a manageable God to meet those needs. A God we can keep under wraps, keep in reserve, keep safely tucked away for just the right moment or need. We want a manageable God to take care of our unmanageable needs. We want part of God to keep us warm (44:16), part of God to cook our dinner (44:16), and the remaining part of God to deliver us from our troubles (44:16). That is truly spiritual schizophrenia! In a chapter entitled "The Utilitarian Christ," A.W. Tozer writes concerning this exact thing,

> *I confess to a feeling of uneasiness about this when I observe the questionable things Christ is said to do for people these days. He (Christ) is often recommended as a wonderfully obliging but not too discriminating big brother who delights to help us accomplish our ends, and who further favors us by forbearing to ask any embarrassing questions about the moral and spiritual qualities of those ends... Thus our Lord becomes the Christ of utility, a kind of Aladdin's lamp to do minor miracles in behalf of anyone who summons Him to do his bidding.*

I love his phrase—*"a wonderfully obliging but not too discriminating big brother!"* In actuality what we want is not a God, but a servant. A servant big enough to deliver us but submissive enough to never threaten our lifestyle. But such a Being simply does not exist (except in the health and wealth gospel). Only an unmanageable God is big enough to satisfy our unmanageable needs. And worthy enough to deserve our unrestrained, white-hot adoration. And good enough to entrust the entirety of our being to. Only one such God exists. His name is Jesus.

> **FLASHPOINT**
> A God small enough for us to utilize cannot be big enough for us to worship.

Why the Creation Account?

"In the beginning God created the heavens and the earth."
Gen. 1:1

Young earth or *old* earth? Did God create in literal twenty-four hour time periods or simply in extended periods of time? My guess is that until Jesus returns, good and godly men and women will continue to hold to both views. Until then, tempers will continue to fly, arguments will continue to become heated, and relationships among fellow Christians will continue to unnecessarily become strained. And at last, our Lord will return and everyone will shake hands and wonder why in the world they had used up so much firepower debating one another (which left them with so little firepower for blessing the vast multitudes outside the family of God). And my strong suspicion is that when Christ returns, the most important issue at stake will not

be being *right,* but being *near.* When we at last see Him
face to face, when—as never before—we behold Him Who
is altogether lovely, when every fiber of our being is elec-
trified by His resplendent glory, I think proving that our
view on the age of the earth was right will seem ludicrous
beyond words. If it turns out we were right, we will simply
shrug and go back to worshipping. If it turns out we were
wrong, we will be glad that the others were right and go
back to worshipping.

Is there a place for dialogue and even debate on the
subject of old vs. new earth? Of course. Graciously, kindly,
respectfully. But I think there is a very important issue at
stake here that seems to be overlooked. Genesis 1 was not
written to provide scientific information but to restrain idolatry. Moses wrote Genesis through Deuteronomy in prepa-
ration for God's people to enter the Promised Land. Once
in the land, they would be tempted to forsake the only true
God and worship the false gods of the Canaanites, Hittites,
etc. Every created entity in Gen. 1 was worshipped as a god
in the land they were about to enter. The sun, moon, stars,
creeping things, great sea creatures, etc. were all gods in
the pagan pantheon of the day. In essence, Moses is writing
Genesis 1 to warn and remind his people of the utter folly of
by-passing the true God to worship things that owed their
very existence to Him in the first place. As Paul put it, *"They
exchanged the truth of God for a lie, and worshiped and served created things rather than the Creator—who is forever praised. Amen."*
(Rom. 1:25). Gleason Archer writes,

The purpose of Genesis 1 is not to tell how fast God performed His work of creation (though, of course, some of His acts, such as the creation of light on the first day, must have been instantaneous). Rather, its true purpose was to reveal that the Lord God who had revealed Himself to the Hebrew race and entered into personal covenant relationship with them was indeed the only true God, the Creator of all things that are.

Our gods tend to not be things created by God, but the works of *our own* hands—materialism, hedonism, egotism, etc. But these gods are no less deadly to our spiritual vitality and health. And we need Genesis 1 every bit as much as they did. But not primarily because of the scientific data it gives, though we certainly avail ourselves to what is there. We need it because it and the rest of the Bible screams to us that we are created beings with a God-shaped hole in our heart which no other created being or thing can fill. That there is a living, loving Creator Who has stepped into human history with track marks that can never be erased. And that if we'll let Him, He'll step into our own lives in the same way. Hard to put it better than Augustine when he wrote, *"Thou hast made us for Thyself, and our hearts are restless until they find their rest in Thee."* May God grant that we settle for nothing less. Just as Genesis 1 reminds us.

FLASHPOINT
Worship, not debate is the purpose of the creation account.

Why Life is not Life

"In Him was life; and the life was the light of men." Jn.1:4

One can never find life in life. And those who seek to do so inevitably will find themselves disappointed. What is popularly called *"life"* among mere mortals is really nothing more than *"existence."* Being born, growing up, gaining an education, finding a job, marrying, raising a family, having sex, eating, drinking, playing a sport, enjoying a hobby, etc.; these are all wonderful components of our temporary pilgrimage on this planet. But none of them have the capacity to provide life. Happiness maybe, pleasure perhaps, but never life.

The reason is simple. God has rigged this thing we call *"life."* Rigged it so that the best life has to offer is never big enough to fill the God-shaped vacuum in our souls. Rigged it so that men and women created in the image of God can never be fully satisfied by anything less than the presence of God. Animals can, but never people. *"In Him was life…"* is God's proclamation of His absolute intolerance. Intolerance of ever allowing what is truly life to be experienced apart from the Supreme Life-giver.

You will show me the path of life; in Your presence is fullness of joy; at Your right hand are pleasures forevermore. Ps. 16:11

Whom have I in heaven but You? And there is none upon earth that I desire besides You. Ps.73:25

How precious is Your lovingkindness, O God! Therefore the children of men put their trust under the shadow of Your wings. They are abundantly satisfied with the fullness of Your house, and You give them drink from the river of Your pleasures. For with You is the fountain of life; in Your light we see light. Ps. 36:7-9

Jonathan Edwards put it so well:

God is the highest good of the reasonable creature, and the enjoyment of him is the only happiness with which our souls can be satisfied.—To go to heaven fully to enjoy God, is infinitely better than the most pleasant accommodations here. Fathers and mothers, husbands, wives, children, or the company of earthly friends, are but shadows. But the enjoyment of God is the substance. These are but scattered beams, but God is the sun. These are but streams, but God is the fountain. These are but drops, but God is the ocean.

The problem with trying to find life in life is that it is truly mistaking the sun-beam for the sun, and the tributary for the ocean. And, as Edwards says, this is shadowy living at best.

FLASHPOINT
Life is never found in life. Don't settle for less than God's best—Him.

Highs and Lows

"Sing to the LORD! Praise the LORD! For He has delivered the life of the poor from the hand of evildoers. Cursed be the day in which I was born! Let the day not be blessed in which my mother bore me!" Jer. 20:13-14

I love this passage. Jeremiah, in the span of two verses, goes from the height of the heights to the depth of the depths. *"Sing to the Lord...Cursed be the day I was born."* Walking with God is a highly unpredictable enterprise, and it inevitably includes vacillating between high delight and deep discouragement. Sometimes, in a second's notice. I am so grateful for the record of saints like Abraham, Job, David, Jeremiah, Elijah, Isaiah, Peter, Paul, etc. They remind us in no uncertain terms that spirituality is not a *destination* but a *journey*. A journey of highs and lows, victories and defeats, good days and bad. And until we hit heaven, *"Sing to the Lord"* and *"Cursed be the day I was born"* will walk hand in hand with all of us.

Anne Bradstreet was America's first woman writer to be published. She lived from 1612-1672. A devout Puritan, her faith was the central driving force of her life as her writings so clearly reflect. I particularly appreciate her raw honesty about walking with God. In a letter to her children she writes,

> *I have had great experience of God's hearing my Prayers, and returning comfortable Answers to me, either in granting the Thing*

I prayed for, or else in satissfying my mind without it; and I have been confident it hath been from him, because I have found my heart through his goodnes enlarged in Thankfulnes to him.

I have often been perplexed that I have not found that constant Joy in my Pilgrimage and refreshing which I supposed most of the servants of God have; although he hath not left me altogether without the wittnes of his holy spirit...Yet have I many Times sinkings and droopings, and not enjoyed that felicity that som- times I have done.

This godly woman follows in the line of Jeremiah— "*I have had great experience of God's hearing my Prayers...I have often been perplexed...*" And so do all of God's choice servants. Like you.

FLASHPOINT
Until we hit heaven, highs and lows will be part and parcel of walking with God. Weather the lows, but don't beat yourself up over them.

The Barnyard

"... these are the ones who have heard the word, and the cares of the world, and the deceitfulness of riches, and the lusts for other things enter in and choke the word, and it becomes unfruitful." Mark 4:18-19

Notice the slow progression—*"enter in and choke."* Ever so slowly but ever so surely, the attractions of this present age drain our spiritual lifeblood if we do not recognize what is happening to us. Danish philosopher Søren Kierkegaard created a parable to illustrate the slow erosion this world can have on our soul. It is the story of a wild duck flying northwards in the spring with all his fellow ducks. The Reverend Andrew Stirling describes it for us:

As they got over Denmark, which was Kierkegaard's home, they decided to land and take a respite. They landed in a farmyard where there were domestic ducks that had become part of the farm experience. This wild duck decided to take it upon himself to eat with these domestic ducks, and filled himself with food. He loved the life on the farm. Every day somebody actually brought food for you! Can you imagine that? There was a warm barn to go into at night with hay for bedding and other animals for company. This is great, thought the duck.

So, he ate more and more and more, and when it came time for his flock to fly off, the duck said, 'Oh, actually, I would like to stay here a little while longer. Why don't the rest of you continue with your migration?' He thought, I am going to sit here and eat and get fat. So, he did.

On their way back south in the fall, the other ducks flew overhead and quacked and made noises and invited their friend to come back. But he said, 'No, I am happy here. I am well fed. I have water, a barn, friends, I don't need to go with you.' But then, he thought about it and decided that maybe he should go. He started to take off, but he was so fat he could only make it as far as the top of the barn. Finally, his wings gave out, and he dropped back down again.

The next spring, the flock came back again. All his friends were in the air, and they all called out, 'Come, come and join us.'

This time, he tried to fly, and he couldn't even get above the door. He was so fat, so happy, so complacent, and so his friends went on to their adventure in the north. Year after year, they flew overhead and invited him to join them, but he didn't. He couldn't move any more. After a while, he didn't even hear them or recognize them, and then he died.

This world, with all that it has to offer, is still—at its best—a barnyard. An attractive barnyard. A pleasurable barnyard. A comfortable barnyard. A sometimes opulent barnyard. But a barnyard is a barnyard is a barnyard. And we are all created for something far grander, far more breathtaking, and infinitely far more significant than barnyard living. We are made to soar on high, to breathe

the crisp and rarified air of knowing God intimately, and to become holy rebels for God's kingdom. To refuse the allure of the barnyard so that we can passionately rise to take hold of our highest calling—to know Him and make Him known. Whatever the cost. Wherever the barnyard.

> **FLASHPOINT**
> We are made for far greater pursuits than barnyard enjoyment. Take flight today.

The Inescapability of Worship

"...and worshipped and served the creature rather than the Creator Who is blessed forever. Amen." Rom.1:25

The root cause of idolatry is something good. Something very good. It is the inescapable reality that God has created all people to be worshippers. Within every one of us is an innate, inextinguishable yearning to adore, revere, and find transcendent satisfaction. No exceptions. Men may deny this reality, stiff arm it, or divert it, but they can never escape it. Because it is such a strong undercurrent of the soul, it will sweep us along in one direction or another. Thus Paul notes that when men turn their back on worshipping God, they *still* worship. *"...and worshipped and served the creature...."* All people are relentless worshippers; it is only a question of the object they worship.

Therefore, sin is always the mismanagement of something very good. It is taking a God-given longing which refuses to be indefinitely put on hold and going in a God-absent direction for its fulfillment. As Augustine put it, *"Sin is energy in the wrong channel."* Through His prophet Jeremiah, God describes it like this: *"For My people have committed two evils: they have forsaken Me, the fountain of living waters, and hewn themselves cisterns—broken cisterns that can hold no water."* (Jer.2:13). The Israelites had taken the legitimate thirst God placed within them and sought to quench it at watering holes that contained nothing of God—broken cisterns. Something we all do on a daily basis.

What is it that we thirst for and hunger after? I like to put it like this: we thirst for a love that cannot be lost or even diminished by our performance, and we hunger to make an impact in life that cannot fade or be erased over time. *Relationship* and *impact* as Dr. Larry Crabb puts it. These are incredibly strong, God-implanted currents within each of us that *will* move us in one direction or another. Either towards God or a broken cistern.

Therefore, dealing with sin is a far deeper proposition than merely staying away from the wrong things. That is like telling a starving man not to eat junk food. We *must* look to see where the legitimate, God-catered banquet resides and seek to feast unreservedly there. John Eldridge put it well when he said, *"What we have left is a Christianity of tips and techniques…It does not take your breath away, and if Christianity does not take your breath away, something else will."* That something else inevitably will be a broken cistern of one variety or another—materialism, illicit sexuality, egotism, co-dependency, or even possibly ministry.

Scottish writer George MacDonald once made the daring assertion, *"When a man knocks at a brothel, he is really knocking for God."* I believe he is absolutely correct. It is more than greed, lust, sensuality, etc. that propels us toward idolatry and sin. Lurking beneath all these maladies is another crucial issue that must be taken into account—the worship factor. If we do not allow the cry of our soul for worship to be answered by God, we *will* begin dialing other numbers. But none of those numbers can deliver what they offer. Augustine was right, *"You have made us for Yourself, and our hearts are restless until they find their rest in You."* Worship is ultimately the best or worst thing we have going for us. Its inescapably will drive us either deeper into the arms of God... or those of His rivals. The choice, of course, is ours.

> **FLASHPOINT**
> May the worship factor in our lives lead us to the worship Source of the universe.

Longevity
FIRE'S TENACITY

"If, after my removal, anyone should think it worth his while to write my life, I will give you a criterion by which you may judge its correctness. If he will give me credit for being a plodder, he will describe me justly. Anything beyond this will be too much. I can plod. I can persevere in any definite pursuit. To this I owe everything."

– WILLIAM CAREY –

K eep the fire burning. *This oft used phrase can refer to many things. It is used in reference to marriage and romance, to staying motivated in a sport or other disciplines, to cooking, and even sustaining creative energy as an entrepreneur. Whatever the use, the underlying meaning is patently clear. It is one thing to get a fire started; it is a very different thing to keep it going. Especially over a long period of time.*

In the spiritual life, it is one thing to begin well. It is a very different thing to finish well. In the parable of the soils, only one soil finished well—the one that persevered. "But the ones that fell on the good ground are those who, having heard the word with a noble and good heart, keep it and bear fruit with patience." *(Lk.8:15). It is almost impossible to overestimate the value and importance of the two words* "with patience." *It is only* "with patience" *that we overcome the trials of life, that we endure the heartaches of disappointment, that we fulfill many mundane responsibilities, that we weather the storms of relationships, that we show up when nobody is watching or cares, that we refuse to let failure be final—and as the writer of Hebrews puts it, that we* "run with endurance the race that is set before us." *(Heb. 12:1). These devotions are devoted to what Eugene Peterson aptly calls* "a long obedience in the same direction." *In other words, God-honoring and God-empowered tenacity.*

Life's one string

"The spirit of a man will sustain his infirmity; but a wounded spirit who can bear?" Pr. 18:14

"A merry heart does good, like medicine, but a broken spirit dries the bones." Pr. 17:22

Who can possibly overestimate the power of a good and godly attitude? Or the devastating consequences of a bad one? I love the way Eugene Peterson translates Pr.18:14 in The Message: *"A healthy spirit conquers adversity, but what can you do when the spirit is crushed?"* Indeed, *"what can you do"* when the one string that has the most power to make or break our lives is frayed or broken? Scott Hamilton, the world famous figure skater and cancer survivor put it so well when he said, *"The only disability in life is a bad attitude."*

There are really very few things we are in complete control of. We like to think that with enough planning, enough strategy, enough diligence, enough perseverance, enough finances, etc. we can gain control of the things we really want. But live long enough, and we all discover the folly of that belief. But what we are in complete control of is our most important possession—*attitude*. Charles Swindoll writes:

The longer I live, the more I realize the impact of attitude on life. Attitude, to me, is more important than facts. It is more important than the past, the education, the money, than circumstances, than failure, than successes, than what other people think or say or do. It is more important than appearance, giftedness or skill. It will make or break a company... a church... a home. The remarkable thing is we have a choice everyday regarding the attitude we will embrace for that day. We cannot change our past... we cannot change the fact that people will act in a certain way. We cannot change the inevitable. The only thing we can do is play on the one string we have, and that is our attitude. I am convinced that life is 10% what happens to me and 90% of how I react to it. And so it is with you... we are in charge of our attitudes.

I love his line, *"We cannot change our past... we cannot change the fact that people will act in a certain way. We cannot change the inevitable. The only thing we can do is play on the one string we have, and that is our attitude."* Attitude may only be one string, but oh what a melody it is capable of playing! This is why we must guard it, nurture it, cultivate it, exploit it. Nothing can more vitalize our spirits, more bring Technicolor to our world, more transform our view of circumstances, than this one string above all strings. Churchill was exactly right: *"Attitude is a little thing that makes a big difference."* I highly recommend that we all take advantage of it! Through God's strength, of course.

FLASHPOINT
The most important change is almost always a change of attitude.

Refusing to Stay "Throwed"

"Indeed we count them blessed who endure. You have heard of the perseverance of Job and seen the end intended by the Lord..." Jas.5:11

Job is forever immortalized by his perseverance. And rightly so. Just a cursory reading of the book of Job leaves all of us wondering how we would have handled his trials. Job's *"end intended by the Lord"* is indeed a marvelous conclusion, but getting there was no walk in the park. A walk through Hades was much more like it. Yet Job continued to put one boil-infested foot in front of another and hung on until he persevered to the end. Is it possible to overestimate the power of perseverance?

But what exactly is this thing called perseverance? The Greek word for it—*hupomone*—was used to describe a plant that being crushed underfoot again and again, continued to rise back up. What a great way to illustrate it! It is the relentless rising again in spite of repeated crushing. William Barclay puts it so well:

> *Hupomone is one of the noblest of NT words...It is the spirit which can bear things, not simply with resignation, but with blazing hope; it is...the spirit which bears things because it knows that these things are leading to a goal of glory; it is not the patience which grimly waits for the end, but the patience which radiantly hopes for the dawn.*

How well put!

The following account of Andrew Jackson from *Our Daily Bread* is a great example of this:

The story is told that Andrew Jackson's boyhood friends just couldn't understand how he became a famous general and then the President of the United States. They knew of other men who had greater talent but who never succeeded. One of Jackson's friends said, 'Why, Jim Brown, who lived right down the pike from Jackson, was not only smarter but he could throw Andy three times out of four in a wrestling match. But look where Andy is now.'

Another friend responded, 'How did there happen to be a fourth time? Didn't they usually say three times and out?' 'Sure, they were supposed to, but not Andy. He would never admit he was beat—he would never stay 'throwed.' Jim Brown would get tired, and on the fourth try Andrew Jackson would throw him and be the winner.' Picking up on that idea, someone has said, 'The thing that counts is not how many times you are 'throwed,' but whether you are willing to stay 'throwed.'

I love that! None of us makes it through life without being *"throwed."* Often severely and usually many, many times. The great issue at stake is whether we will *"stay throwed,"* or will get up and step back into the ring. May God grant each of us the grace and ability to specialize in ring re-entry, difficult as it usually is. Job cries out to us from his ringside seat, *"It will be so worth it, don't stay throwed!"*

> **FLASHPOINT**
> Refuse to stay "throwed." God's not through with you.

Refusing to Allow Failure to be Final

"For a righteous man may fall seven times and rise again..." Pr.24:16

One of the most difficult facets of endurance is the ability to move forward after personal failure. There is something uniquely discouraging and defeating about falling into a ditch that we have dug for ourselves. There is a shadow cast by sins and mistakes of one's own foolish doings that relentlessly seeks to cloud and obscure any possibilities for usefulness in the future. This passage in Proverbs is a great encouragement to me, as I hope it is to you. Apparently, the mark of a righteous man is not that he makes it through life without stumbling (Jas.3:2). Nor is it that he very rarely falls—*"Seven times"* essentially means "innumerable times" in biblical terminology. The mark of a righteous man is that he refuses to let failure be final. I love the true story Haddon Robinson relates:

New Year's Day, 1929, Georgia Tech played University of California in the Rose Bowl. In that game a man named Roy Riegels recovered a fumble for California. Somehow, he became confused and started running 65 yards in the wrong direction. One of his teammates, Benny Lom, outdistanced him and downed him just before he scored for the opposing team. When California attempted to punt, Tech blocked the kick and scored a safety which was the ultimate margin of victory. That strange play came in the first half, and everyone who was watching the game was asking the same question: 'What will Coach Nibbs Price do with Roy Riegels in the second half?' The men filed off the field and went into the dressing room. They sat down on the benches and on the floor, all but Riegels. He put his blanket around his shoulders, sat down in a corner, put his face in his hands, and cried like a baby.

If you have played football, you know that a coach usually has a great deal to say to his team during half time. That day Coach Price was quiet. No doubt he was trying to decide what to do with Riegels. Then the timekeeper came in and announced that there were three minutes before playing time. Coach Price looked at the team and said simply, 'Men the same team that played the first half will start the second.' The players got up and started out, all but Riegels. He did not budge. The coach looked back and called to him again; still he didn't move. Coach Price went over to where Riegels sat and said, 'Roy, didn't you hear me? The same team that played the first half will start the second.' Then Roy Riegels looked up and his cheeks were wet with a strong man's tears. 'Coach,' he said, 'I can't do it to save my life. I've ruined you, I've ruined the University of California, I've ruined myself. I couldn't face that crowd in the stadium to save my life.' Then Coach Price reached out and put his hand on Riegel's shoulder and said to him: 'Roy, get up and go on back; the game is only half over.' And Roy Riegels went back, and those Tech men will tell you that they have never seen a man play football as Roy Riegels played that second half.

Every one of us is or has been a Roy Riegels in the first half. The great question is whether we will be the Roy Riegels of the second half. *"For a righteous man may fall seven times"*...but he or she still gets up, goes out, and plays the second half with abandon. For the glory of God.

FLASHPOINT
Refuse to allow failure to be final. The second half is waiting for you.

Never Too Late

"They shall still bear fruit in old age; they shall be fresh and flourishing." Ps.92:14

It is never too late to do something extraordinary with one's life. History records that many people have made their greatest contributions to society after the age of 70. Nelson Mandela became President of South Africa on his 89th birthday. Goethe wrote "Faust" at 82. Galileo made his greatest discovery when he was 73. Harry Bernstein's first book, "The Invisible Wall," came out just weeks before the author's 97th birthday. At 89, Arthur Rubinstein gave one of his greatest recitals in New York's Carnegie Hall. On and on it goes.

Likewise, scripture records that much of God's work was (and is) accomplished through His oldest saints. Caleb took the mountain promised him at 85. Moses began leading God's people into the Promised Land at 80. Abraham and Sarah were way too old to have Isaac, but God seems to not be limited by human years.

Age, for the most part, is truly a state of mind. General Douglas MacArthur put it so well:

Nobody grows old by merely living a number of years. People grow old only by deserting their ideals. Years may wrinkle the skin, but to give up interest wrinkles the soul. Worry, doubt, self-distrust, fear and despair—these are the long, long years that bow the head and turn the growing spirit back to dust. Whatever your years, there is in every being's heart the love of wonder, the un-daunted challenge of events, the unfailing childlike appetite for what next, and the joy and the game of life.

You are as young as your faith, as old as your doubt; as young as your self-confidence, as old as your fear; as young as your hope, as old as your despair. In the central place of every heart there is a recording chamber; so long as it receives messages of beauty, hope, cheer and courage, so long are you young. When the wires are all down and your heart is covered with the snows of pessimism and the ice of cynicism, then, and then only are you grown old—and then, indeed, as the ballad says, you just fade away.

Few sights are more compellingly attractive and inspiring than white haired saints who are *"fresh and flourishing,"* who *"still bear fruit in old age."* To see someone still taking risks at the end of their days, refusing to allow their inner being to enter into retirement, relentlessly climbing to higher and higher ground...this person inspires more hope and dispenses more motivation than they have any idea.

FLASHPOINT
Keep climbing higher. There is no such thing as a retired saint.

The Power of Plodding

"...Let us run with endurance the race that is set before us," Heb.12:1

William Carey translated the Bible into over forty different Indian dialects from 1793 to 1834. Though he never graduated from even high school, Carey became one of the greatest linguists the world has ever known. This Englishman overcame tremendous obstacles and setbacks during his years in India. One of his children died, his wife became mentally ill, death threats were made against him, his home and much of his translation work were destroyed in a great fire. He ministered for seven years before he saw his first convert. Shortly before he died, he gave out his secret for success to his sister Eunice:

If, after my removal, anyone should think it worth his while to write my life, I will give you a criterion by which you may judge its correctness. If he will give me credit for being a plodder, he will describe me justly. Anything beyond this will be too much. I can plod. I can persevere in any definite pursuit. To this I owe everything.

"I can plod...To this I owe everything." The older I get, the more I appreciate those words. When I was young, starry-eyed, and starting out in ministry I had no idea:

...That life would be so hard so much of the time.

...That temptations would not diminish as I got older...

in fact, they would often seem to get worse.

...That criticisms would sting as badly at 57 as at 27.

...That failure would be a closer companion than I ever expected.

...That I would have more questions about God and the life of faith towards the end of my life than at the beginning.

...That some of my closest companions would one day become some of my most outspoken critics.

...That walking away from the faith would be appealing at times.

But this one thing I have become increasingly convinced of—there is no way to overestimate the value, power, and impact of simply *"plodding."* Of simply putting one foot in front of the next, no matter how painfully or falteringly, knowing it is leading to a better place. Never a perfect place. But a place that infinitely beats the alternative— throwing in the towel. As Calvin wrote, *"it is better to limp in the way, than run with the greatest swiftness out of it."* Perseverance through God's infused power enables us to move forward, slow as it may be, in the only race which truly matters. And, like Carey, we too will one day echo the words, *"I can plod...to this I owe everything."*

FLASHPOINT
A small, faltering step forward is still progress.

The Common Task

"And whatever you do, do it heartily, as to the Lord and not to men, knowing that from the Lord you will receive the reward of the inheritance; for you serve the Lord Christ." Col. 3:23-24

The word *"routine"* comes from a Latin root which essentially means *"a beaten path."* Hence we also get the word *"route"* from the same root. And this is a good way to describe so very much of our lives. It is the beaten path of doing common, every day, mundane things over and over and over...and then yet over again. Washing the dishes, mowing the lawn, making dinner, changing diapers, paying bills, etc. all are part of the routine of dynamic, vibrant Christianity. Yes— dynamic, vibrant, all-out spirituality. Even when the doing of these things doesn't seem to make any difference. Dr. Martin Luther King spoke these powerful words to sanitation workers in Memphis one month before he was assassinated:

> *All labor has value. If you're a street sweeper, sweep streets the way Michelangelo painted pictures. Sweep streets the way Beethoven composed music. Sweep streets the way Shakespeare wrote poetry. Sweep streets in such a profound way that the Host of Heaven will say, 'There goes a great street sweeper'*

Just because something is *routine* doesn't mean that it is *insignificant*. Far from it. According to Paul, as the bondservants planted the crops, fed the livestock, scrubbed the floors, etc. with their whole hearts as unto the Lord; they were laying up treasure in heaven for every seemingly mundane task. And so are you.

British pastor F.B. Meyer put it so well:

Knitting needles are cheap and common enough, but on them may be wrought the fairest designs in the richest wools. So the incidents of daily life may be commonplace in the extreme, but on them as the material foundation we may build the unseen but everlasting fabric of a noble and beautiful character…What we do may or may not live; but the way in which we perform our common tasks becomes an indestructible part of our character, for better or worse…

We are sent into this world to build up characters which will be blessed and useful in that great future for which we are being trained. There is a niche which only we can fill, a crown which only we can wear, music which only we can waken, service which only we can render…Life is our school house. Its rooms may be bare, but they are littered with opportunities of becoming fit for our great inheritance.

I love his thought, *"Life is our school house. Its rooms may be bare, but they are littered with opportunities of becoming fit for our great inheritance."* Yes, the seemingly small things in this life do matter. They matter now, and they matter for all eternity. And most likely, we won't fully understand how much they mattered until we enter eternity. Until then, we take it by faith. And perform the common task as if all the saints and angels of heaven were watching. And they are.

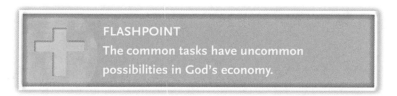

FLASHPOINT
The common tasks have uncommon possibilities in God's economy.

Just Show Up

"Be ready in season and out of season..." II Tim. 4:2

Ours is not to decide when we will be most useful to God. As if we trafficked in that kind of omniscience in the first place. Ours is to *"be ready."* The word Paul uses here was used in Greek literature to describe a soldier *"staying at his post."* The soldier of Christ is to stay at his post, to simply remain doggedly faithful to the present task at hand. And then Paul adds the intriguing phrase *"in season and out of season."* This probably has the thought of *"when it is convenient and when it is inconvenient."* But it also points out a critical truth concerning usefulness and ministry.

Our calling is not to recognize the time of our usefulness, but to just keep showing up, showing up, showing up. Showing up to love God with all of our being. Showing up to love the brethren on good days and bad. Showing up to reach out into a needy broken world with the love of Christ regardless of how we think they will respond. Showing up for daily, routine, unglamorous faithfulness in our homes and at our jobs. And it is in the pathway of just daily, hourly showing up that God uses His people in ways far beyond anything they might imagine.

The poverty-stricken widow just showed up, faithfully deposited her meager two mites, and went her way (Lk. 21:1-4). Could she possibly have known the influence her showing up would have for the next 2,000 years?

The publican just showed up. In brokenness and humility he prayed, *"God, be merciful to me, sinner"* (Lk. 18:13). Could he have possibly known the ways God would use his showing up and prayer over the next 2,000 years? Of course not. And neither do any of us know how God is going to use our most common, seemingly insignificant steps to love Him and influence others. What we do know is that God delights to use His people when they least expect it. All they do is show up.

An unnamed woman with a very checkered past just showed up. She washed Christ's feet with her tears, wiped them with her hair, kissed them, and anointed them with fragrant oil. (Lk.7:36-50) Could she possibly have known the now 2,000 year impact her unreserved and unrestrained gratitude would have on untold numbers of lives? Or that Christ would use her as an object lesson as to why Simon and the rest of the Pharisees loved so little? Of course not. She just showed up.

It has been said, *"Satan doesn't care what we do for God, as long as we do it tomorrow."* So, so true. And one of Satan's most deceptive strategies is to get us focusing on our usefulness in the future so as to distract us from our faithfulness in the present. That way myriads of opportunities for present impact are forfeited while we concern ourselves with how God is going to use us next. Fact is, none of us really has the foggiest idea how God is going to use us next. Far, far better to stay dialed in to this day, this hour, this moment. It is, after all, the only time frame we are guaranteed.

> **FLASHPOINT**
> Just show up, God will take care of the useful part. Astonishingly good care.

Obscure Obedience

"Now Moses was tending the flock of Jethro...And he led the flock to the back of the desert and Angel of the Lord appeared to him..." Exodus 3:1-2

She was just trying to get home from a long day at work. There was nothing premeditated or pre-planned. As she later stated, *"I did not get on the bus to get arrested. I got on the bus to go home."* Yet on Dec.1, 1955 aboard the Cleveland Avenue bus in Montgomery, Alabama our world was changed. An extraordinary response on a very ordinary day helped spark long awaited and overdue changes in racial segregation. The response? Refusing to give up her seat to a white man. A simple act of quiet fortitude on an ordinary city bus in an ordinary American city on an ordinary winter day. Who would ever have dreamed that her humble but courageous response would trigger the avalanche that it did? As Rosa Parks herself remarked, *"At the time I was arrested I had no idea it would turn into this. It was just a day like any other day. The only thing that made it significant was that the masses of the people joined in."*

Ah, the power of obscure obedience! I'm particularly drawn to Rosa's statement, *"It was just a day like any other day..."* I'm sure Moses would have said exactly the same thing about the day that so markedly and profoundly changed the direction of his life. Just an ordinary day like any other day on the backside of the desert. Doing what he did almost everyday...until God intersected and interrupted his routine. Tending the flock of Jethro would be exchanged for tending the flock of God.

We never know when our greatest opportunities for impacting others and society will come knocking. The moments that most profoundly mark our lives are rarely expected. They sneak up behind us, come upon us in an instant, and require an immediate response one way or the other. And most often, they come to us on *"a day just like any other day."* For this reason one of my firm convictions is that there really is no such thing as an ordinary day. Every day is pregnant with opportunities for godly, extraordinary living. Small, quiet acts of care towards the less fortunate. Humble, gracious responses to mistreatment. Courageous, spontaneous movement into a difficult situation. Helen Keller put it well, *"I long to accomplish a great and noble task, but it is my chief duty to accomplish humble tasks as though they were great and noble."*

An ordinary bus, an ordinary city, an ordinary day, an ordinary person. But one extraordinary response and society would never be the same. Therefore, as we go through the day let us depend upon the Lord not merely to be great *doers*, but especially great *responders*. One never knows where an extraordinary response on an ordinary day will lead. Or the latent power of quiet, humble, obscure faithfulness. Martin Luther put it so well, *"The maid who sweeps her kitchen is doing the will of God just as much as the monk who prays—not because she may sing a Christian hymn as she sweeps but because God loves clean floors."* I love that thought.

FLASHPOINT
Obscure obedience on earth is headline news in heaven. Count on it.

Conclusion

Keep the Flame Burning

A nd so my friend, we come to the end of our journey.
At least for the time being. I hope that you have discovered the Fire within you kindled afresh many times
throughout your reading of these short reflections. If this
has happened, then truly the writing of this book will have
been worth all the effort. Where then, do we go from here?

I began our journey with these words, *"This book is founded upon one central, bedrock conviction:* **There is a permanent,
inextinguishable fire in every believer's soul.** *A God-birthed
fire…a Spirit-sustained fire…a Christ-adoring fire. It is a holy fire,
a gifted fire for which we can take no credit. Its flames can never be
fully doused; regardless of the amount of sin, rebellion, confusion, or
idolatry in our lives. This fire yearns to enflame every facet of our
being but will not go where it is not invited. It is a gentle fire. It
is a kind fire. But make no mistake; it is also a jealous fire. A fire
that violently protests every vestige of sin in our lives while deeply
delighting in our every small, faltering movement towards the Lover
of our souls."*

I believe this with every fiber of my being. And that's
why you, my dear reader, are dangerous. So very, very dangerous. Dangerous to the arch-enemy of our souls and his
sordid, deceitful ploys to destroy men's lives and usurp the
true King's authority. Let me explain.

There resides within you the very life and fire of Jesus

Christ Himself. The Warrior of warriors has taken up glad residence in the citadel of your soul. Once you allow the draw-bridge of your life to be lowered, He will be on the march to *"to preach good tidings to the poor...to heal the broken-hearted...to proclaim liberty to the captives...and the opening of the prison to those who are bound."* (Isaiah 61:1) The Spirit of the living God within you is restlessly awaiting the opening of your floodgates so that He can rush forth to make much of Jesus through you. You have more to offer than you have any idea. You are more dangerous than you have ever imagined. Yes...*you.*

You-- with all your faults and demons. You—with all your past failures and soul-smothering guilt. You --with all your carefully concealed scars and wounds of abuse. You—with all your raging lusts, hidden insecurities, and cleverly disguised forms of arrogance. You—who have tried to head-fake God time and again, but to no avail. You—who feel cold toward God more often than you would want anyone to know, who have at times considered walking away from the whole thing, and who are convinced that you're just not the kind of material God could ever really use. Guess what? You are not alone. Not by a long shot. *Every* (and I mean every) honest Christian knows that they are card-carrying members of this exact same club that I have just described. A club whose members only have one thing going for them—overflowing, indwelling grace.

The reason any of us are dangerous is not what we bring to the Fire. It's what the Fire brings to us. Or better, what the Fire brings through us. Being dangerous is not a matter of gritting our teeth, cleaning up our act, and trying our best to serve our Lord. It is a matter of falling back in desperate dependency upon a Fire not our own to produce a light and warmth not our own for a glory not our own. *"I will not dare to speak of anything except what Christ has accomplished through me in word and in deed resulting in the obedience of the Gentiles."* (Romans 15:18) is Paul's summary of the effectiveness of his life. In other words, when we allow the Fire to kindle within us, it shines from us.

That my friend, is your calling. Your opportunity. Your ticket to a life that outstrips all the shallow pleasures and trivial honors known to man. But for this Fire to be released through you it must be nurtured within you. At all costs, take the time to kindle this fire within. Nothing matters more. Then abandon yourself in glad surrender to the greatest privilege and opportunity available to men and women on this planet—becoming flesh and blood "kindling for the Fire". Kindling for that Fire who burns both furiously and gently, thunderously and quietly, dangerously and safely. Nothing matters more. Nothing satisfies more. And nothing, but nothing, glorifies our King more. May God grant we settle for nothing less.

BIBLIOGRAPHY

INTRODUCTION

1. "What fire is this that warms my soul?": Augustine of Hippo, translated by Boniface Ramsey, *Soliloquies: Augustine's Inner Dialogue* (Hyde Park, N.Y.: New City Press, 1999), 35

2. "Our God is a consuming fire" – Heb. 12:29

3. "sealed by the Holy Spirit" – Eph. 4:30

RADIANCE—FIRE'S BEAUTY

4. "Life has loveliness to sell": Sara Teasdale, *Barter*, edited by Susan Rattiner, *Great poems by American Women: An Anthology* (Mineola, N.Y.: Dover Publications, 1998), 187

5. "should also be beautiful": Francis Schaeffer, *True Spirituality* (Wheaton, Ill.: Tyndale, 1971), 177

6. "Earth is crammed with heaven": Elizabeth Barrett Browning, *Aurora Leigh*, edited by D.H. Nicholson and A.H.E. Lee, *The Oxford Book of English Mystical Verse* (Oxford: Clarendon Press, 1917), 187

7. "It is to the spirit": Frederick Buechner, as quoted by Luci Shaw, *Breath for the Bones* (Nashville: Thomas Nelson, 2001), 49

8. "God's excellency": Jonathan Edwards, *Personal Narrative* from *The Works of President Edwards*, vol. I, ed. Sereno B. Dwight, 1830

9. "Then suddenly there dawns": Paul Tournier, *Guilt and Grace*, trans. Arthur W. Heathcote (San Francisco: Harper & Row, 1983), 193

10. "It is easy to think": C.S. Lewis, *Mere Christianity* (New York: HarperCollins, 2001), 199.

11. "I believe it is a grave mistake": Dorothy L. Sayers, "Creed or Chaos" *The Whimsical Christian* (New York: Macmillan, 1978), 34-5.

12. "And what do I love…": Augustine, *The Confessions of Saint Augustine* (Grand Rapids: Baker Book House, 1977), 18

13. "Here then I am, far from the busy ways of men": John Wesley, *Selections from the Writings of the Rev. John Wesley* (New York, The Methodist Book Concern, 1901), 14

14. "Every young student knows": C.S. Kirkendall, http://www.sermonillustrations.com/a-z/s/selflessness.htm

15. "I went to Africa": Henry Stanley on David Livingstone, as quoted by Ruth A. Tucker, *From Jerusalem to Irian Jaya* (Grand Rapids, Mich.: Zondervan, 1983), 153

16. "I would like to take this opportunity": Ward Goodrich, *Our Daily Bread* http://odb.org/1994/03/22/why-did-this-happen/

17. "The Church's approach to an intelligent carpenter": Dorothy L. Sayers, "Creed or Chaos" *The Whimsical Christian* (New York: Macmillan, 1978), .

FRAGRANCE—FIRE'S AROMA

18. "Spirituality is not easy to define": J. Oswald Sanders, *Enjoying Intimacy With God* (Chicago: Moody, 1980), 79

19. "The word **Christian** means different things": Eugene Peterson, *Traveling Light* (Colorado Springs: Helmers & Howard, 1988), 57-58

20. "Imagine yourself as a living house": C.S. Lewis, *The Quotable Lewis*, ed. Wayne Martindale and Jerry Root (Wheaton, Ill.: Tyndale, 1989), 98

21. "Experience: that most brutal of teachers": C.S. Lewis, *The Quotable Lewis*, ed. Wayne Martindale and Jerry Root (Wheaton, Ill.: Tyndale, 1989), 350

22. "I will put courage into thee.": George Bernard Shaw, *Saint Joan* (New York: Penguin, 2001),

23. "From prayer that asks that I may be": Amy Carmichael, *Mountain Breezes* (Harrisburg, Pa.: Christian Literature Crusade, 1999), 74

24. "The first effect of the power of God": Jonathan Edwards, *Religious Affections* (Portland, Ore.: Multnomah, 1984), 8

25. "The Holy Ghost is sent forth": Martin Luther, *Commentary on Galatians*, ed. John Prince Fallowes (Grand Rapids, Mich.: Kregel, 1979), 238

26. "God's respect to the creature's good" Jonathan Edwards, as quoted by John Piper, *God's Passion for His Glory* (Wheaton, Ill.: Crossway,1998), 33

27. "I thank Thee first": Matthew Henry as quoted by Arnold Gingrich, *Coronet*, Volume 17 (1944)

28. "The spiritual leader, however, influences others": J. Oswald Sanders, *Spiritual Leadership* (Chicago: Moody, 1980), 33

29. "There is an absolute and universal dependence": Jonathan Edwards, "Sermon 1: God Glorified in Man's Dependence," *The Works of Jonathan Edwards* (Carlisle, Pa.: Banner of Truth Trust, 1986), 3

THE FIRE TRIANGLE—FIRE'S TRIUMVIRATE

30. "I feel so strongly at the end of my life": Malcom Muggeridge, *The Great Liberal Death Wish*, http://www.malcolmmuggeridge.org/gargoyle/gargoyle-04-200410.pdf

31. "Each human soul is like a cavern full of gems": Cannon Farrar, as

quoted by Henry Southgate, *The Christian Life* (London: Charles Griffin and Sons, 1884), 197

32. "There are two seas in Palestine" Bruce Barton, "There Are Two Seas," *McCall's*, 1928

33. "Hope is one of the Theological virtues": C.S. Lewis, *The Quotable Lewis*, ed. Wayne Martindale and Jerry Root (Wheaton, Ill.: Tyndale, 1989), 305, 306

34. "A traveler is not wont to rest": Jonathan Edwards, *Jonathan Edwards: Basic Writings*, ed. Ola Winslow (New York: Penguin, 1966), 1984

35. "Our Father refreshes us": C.S. Lewis, *The Problem of Pain* (New York: Macmillan, 1962)

FIREWOOD – FIRE'S COMMUNITY

36. "When I first became a Christian": C.S. Lewis, *God in the Dock* (Grand Rapids, Mich.: Eerdmans, 1970), 61-62

37. "General Grant's chief of staff": Clarence E. Macartney, *Macartney's Illustrations* (Nashville, Tenn.: Abingdon, 1946), 136

38. "Christian brotherhood is not an ideal": Dietrich Bonhoeffer, *Life Together* (San Francisco: Harper & Row, 1954), 30

39. "...in all fields, even those of culture and art": Paul Tournier, *Guilt and Grace*, trans. Arthur W. Heathcote (San Francisco: Harper & Row, 1983), 15

40. "Of the Seven Deadly Sins": Frederick Buechner, *Wishful Thinking* (New York: HarperOne, 1973), 3

41. "To forgive is to set a prisoner free": Lewis Smedes, *The Art of Forgiving* (New York: Ballantine Books, 1996), 16

FUEL—FIRE'S RESOURCING

42. "While I was staying at Nailsworth": George Mueller, as quoted by John Piper, *Desiring God* (Portland, Oreg.: Multnomah, 1986), 116

43. "It is a Christian duty": C.S. Lewis from a letter to Sheldon Vanauken in Vanauken's book, *A Severe Mercy* (New York: Harper and Row, 1977), 189.

44. "There once was in man": Blaise Pascal, *Thoughts,* translated by W. F. Trotter. Vol. XLVIII, Part 1. The Harvard Classics. (New York: P.F. Collier & Son, 1909), 202

45. "My principal enjoyment": Henry Martyn, as quoted by John Sargent, *Life and Letters of Henry Martyn* (Carlisle, Pa.: Banner of Truth Trust, 1985), 130

46. "Oh! That I might repose on Thee": Augustine, *The Confessions of Saint Augustine* (Grand Rapids: Baker Book House, 1977), 35,36

47. "Christ is claiming the ability": J. Oswald Sanders, *Spiritual Lessons* (Chicago: Moody, 1971), 184

48. "The bough that breaks off": A.W. Tozer, *The Root of the Righteous* (Harrisburg Pa.: Christian Publications, 1955), 8

49. "thou art so entirely joined unto Christ": Martin Luther, *Commentary on Galatians*, ed. John Prince Fallowes (Grand Rapids, Mich.: Kregel, 1979), 25

50. "Before my conversion": Martin Luther, *Commentary on Galatians*, ed. John Prince Fallowes (Grand Rapids, Mich.: Kregel, 1979), 161

51. "The moment I consider": Martin Luther, *Commentary on Galatians*, ed. John Prince Fallowes (Grand Rapids, Mich.: Kregel, 1979), 79

52. "I never got away from Jesus": David Brainerd, *The Works of Jonathan Edwards* (Carlisle, Pa.: Banner of Truth Trust, 1986), 138

53. "You may be able to compel": Reinhold Niebuhr, as quoted in Charles R. Swindoll, *The Grace Awakening* (Nashville: Word, 1990), 15

54. "If you believe in Jesus": Oswald Chambers, *My Utmost for His Highest* (CD-ROM, United Kingdom: Marshall Morgan & Scott, 1927)

55. "There are two main ways in which": Dr. Martyn Lloyd-Jones, *Joy Unspeakable* (Colorado Springs, Colo.: Shaw, 1984), 18

FLAMES – FIRE'S ESSENCE

56. "God has used a number of": A.W. Tozer, *The Knowledge of the Holy* (New York: HarperCollins, 1961), 43

57. "Then he isn't safe?": C.S. Lewis, *The Quotable Lewis*, ed. Wayne Martindale and Jerry Root (Wheaton, Ill.: Tyndale, 1989), 55

58. "The God of White-Hot Rage": John White, The Race (Downers Grove, Ill.: InterVarsity, 1984),25,33

59. "The vague and tenuous hope": A.W. Tozer, *The Knowledge of the Holy* (New York: HarperCollins, 1961), 59

60. "We regard God": C.S. Lewis, *The Problem of Pain* (New York: Macmillan, 1962), 16

61. "The church of North America": Eugene Nida: As related to me by Walt Baker, missions professor at Dallas Theological Seminary, from a personal conversation with Dr. Nida

62. "An idol is whatever you": Tim Keller, *Counterfeit Gods* (New York: Dutton, 2009), 44

63. "The God of Abraham": A.W. Tozer, *The Knowledge of the Holy* (New York: HarperCollins, 1961), 12

64. "God is a Spirit infinitely happy": Stephen Charnock, *The Existence and Attributes of God* (Grand Rapids, Baker Books,1996), 171

65. "Both for perplexity": William Temple, *Readings in St. John's Gospel* (New York: Morehouse, 1985), 109

66. "While we are looking at God": A.W. Tozer, *The Pursuit of God* (Camp Hill, Pa.: Christian Publications, 1993), 11

THE HEARTH—FIRE'S HOMESTEAD

67. "If New Testament Christianity: J.B. Phillips, *New Testament Christianity* (London: Hodder & Stoughton, 1956), 76

68. "The basis for this tremendous burst": Harry Reasoner, http://www. sermoncentral.com/illustrations/searchresults.asp?keyword=Light%20 Bursts&Pro=1

69. "While it lasts": C.S. Lewis, *The Quotable Lewis*, ed. Wayne Martindale and Jerry Root (Wheaton, Ill.: Tyndale, 1989), 79

70. "You must picture me alone": C.S. Lewis, *The Quotable Lewis*, ed. Wayne Martindale and Jerry Root (Wheaton, Ill.: Tyndale, 1989), 55

71. "The coming of Jesus into the world": Malcolm Muggeridge, *Jesus, The Man Who Lives* (New York: HarperCollins, 1984), 48

72. "For (Alexander Whyte)": C.S. Lewis, *The Quotable Lewis*, ed. Wayne Martindale and Jerry Root (Wheaton, Ill.: Tyndale, 1989), 548

73. "Often, since I lived in this town": Jonathan Edwards, *Jonathan Edwards: Basic Writings*, ed. Ola Winslow (New York: Penguin, 1966), 94

74. "There is nothing small in the Christian": F.B. Meyer as quoted by J. Oswald Sanders in *Spiritual Lessons* (Chicago:Moody,1971), 47

75. "It is my pride": Howard E. Butt, from a talk called *"The Art of Being a Big Shot"* delivered in 1963 at the Layman's Leadership Institute in Dallas, Texas

SPARKS—FIRE'S EMISSARIES

76. "We can all do the heroic thing": Oswald Chambers, *My Utmost for His Highest* (CD-ROM, United Kingdom: Marshall Morgan & Scott, 1927)

77. "For my own part": David Livingstone, as quoted by John Piper, *Desiring God* (Portland, Oreg.: Multnomah, 1986), 201,202

78. "Perhaps you've heard": found at *http://www.crosswalk.com/faith/spiritual-life/an-eternally-consequential-life-1299911.html*

79. "I started down town": John MacArthur, *Twelve Ordinary Men* (Nashville, Tenn.: Thomas Nelson, 2002), 82

80. "Now the range": Henry Jowett, *The School of Calvary* (London: James Clark and Co., 1911), 97

81. "At last, by the mercy of God": Martin Luther, as recorded by Marilyn Harran, *Luther and Learning* (Cranbury, NJ: Associated University Presses, 1985), 38

82. "In the evening": John Wesley, *The Journals of John Wesley* (Chicago: Moody Press, 1974), 98

83. *"Thou canst not,":* Pliny, http://www.calvarycsd.org/sermons/john-1518-25-warning-the-world-hates-you/

84. "We are moved": Samuel Chadwick as recorded by J. Oswald Sanders, *Spiritual Discipleship*(Chicago: Moody Press, 1990), 30

85. "The harlot, the liar, the murderer": H.C.G.Moule, *The Epistle to the Romans* (London: Pickering & Inglis, 1861), 30

LIGHT – FIRE'S BRILLIANCE

86. "I believe in Christianity": C.S. Lewis, *The Quotable Lewis*, ed. Wayne Martindale and Jerry Root (Wheaton, Ill.: Tyndale, 1989), 55

87. "We are constantly assured": Dorothy Sayers, *Letters to a Diminished Church* (Nashville: W. Publishing Group, 2004), 1

88. "If some watcher" A.W. Tozer, *The Knowledge of the Holy* (New York: HarperCollins, 1961), 65

89. "God doesn't explain.": Frederick Buechner, as quoted by Philip Yancey, *Where is God When it Hurts?* (Grand Rapids, Mich.: Zondervan, 1977), 108

90. "First of all": Martin Lloyd-Jones, *Romans, An Exposition of Chapter 6* (Grand Rapids, Mich.: Zondervan, 1972), 8.

91. "If our religion": C.S. Lewis, *The Quotable Lewis*, ed. Wayne Martindale and Jerry Root (Wheaton, Ill.: Tyndale, 1989), 73

92. "I never got away": David Brainerd, *The Works of Jonathan Edwards* (Carlisle, Pa.: Banner of Truth Trust, 1986), 138

93. "The missionary among Moslems": Samuel Zwemer, *The Glory of the Cross* (London:Marshall, Organ, and Scott, 1928), 113

94. "It would be dreadful": Jonathan Edwards, "Sinners in the Hands of an Angry God," *The Works of Jonathan Edwards* (Edinburgh: The Banner of Truth and Trust, 1834), 11.

95. "The maid who sweeps": Martin Luther as recorded by Mark Allen Powell, *Giving to God* (Grand Rapids, Mich.: Eerdmans, 2006), 85

HEAT – FIRE'S WARMTH

96. "Ye angels of God" Elizabeth Rowe, as quoted by Bruce Shelley, *All the Saints Adore Thee* (Grand Rapids, Mich.: Zondervan, 1988), 138

97. "As there is no true religion": Jonathan Edwards, *Religious Affections* (Portland, Ore.: Multnomah, 1984), 17

98. "Here is true Christian mysticism": Francis Schaeffer, *True Spirituality* (Wheaton, Ill.: Tyndale, 1971), 54-55

99. "And what do I love": Augustine, as quoted by Bruce Shelley, *All the Saints Adore Thee* (Grand Rapids, Mich.: Zondervan, 1988), 40.

100. "I have known men": Thomas Goodwin as quoted by J. Oswald Sanders, *Prayer Power Unlimited* (Chicago: Moody Press, 1974), 168

101. "The man who has God": A.W. Tozer, *The Pursuit of God* (Camp Hill, Pa.: Christian Publications, 1993), 40

102. "Has God put you": Oswald Chambers, *My Utmost for His Highest* (CD-ROM, United Kingdom: Marshall Morgan & Scott, 1927

103. "Joy is not a substitute": C.S. Lewis, *The Quotable Lewis*, ed. Wayne Martindale and Jerry Root (Wheaton, Ill.: Tyndale, 1989), 232

104. "It's a bad world": http://www.biblecenter.com/sermons/howtoliveahappylife.htm

105. "Happiness turns up more or less": Frederick Buechner, *Beyond Words* (New York, HarperCollins, 2004), 204

106. "If there lurks": C.S. Lewis, *The Quotable Lewis*, ed. Wayne Martindale and Jerry Root (Wheaton, Ill.: Tyndale, 1989), 273

107. "Beware of an untheological devotion": H.C.G. Moule, *Colossians and Philemon Studies* (Grand Rapids, Mich.:Zondervan, 2002), 55.

108. "We Communists have a high casualty rate": Charles Swindoll, *Man to Man* (Grand Rapids, Mich.: Zondervan, 1996), 223

109. "To those who knew him": Dorothy Sayers, "Creed or Chaos?" *The Whimsical Christian* (New York:Macmillan, 1978), 34-5

SHADOWS—FIRE'S FLICKERING

110. "I have had great experiences": Anne Bradstreet, as recorded by Helen Campbell, *Anne Bradstreet and Her Time* (Middlesex, UK.: The Echo Library, 2007), 217

111. "Meanwhile, where is God?": C.S. Lewis, *The Quotable Lewis*, ed. Wayne Martindale and Jerry Root (Wheaton, Ill.: Tyndale, 1989), 119

112. "I confess to a feeling of uneasiness": A.W. Tozer, *The Root of the Righteous* (Harrisburg Pa.: Christian Publications, 1955), 8

113. "The purpose of Genesis 1": Gleason Archer as recorded in http://www.gci.org/bible/genesis/sixdays

114. "God is the highest good": Jonathan Edwards, *Jonathan Edwards: Basic Writings*, ed. Ola Winslow (New York: Penguin, 1966), 141

115. "I have had great experiences": Anne Bradstreet, as recorded by Helen Campbell, *Anne Bradstreet and Her Time* (Middlesex, UK.: The Echo Library, 2007), 217

LONGEVITY – FIRE'S TENACITY

116. "If, after my removal": William Carey, as found in http://www.wciujournal.org/monthly/article/william-careys-current-contribution-to-bible-translation-wyclipedia

117. "The longer I live": Charles Swindoll, *Strengthening Your Grip* (Nashville, Tenn.: Thomas Nelson, 2003), 131

118. "Hupomone is one of the noblest of NT words": William Barclay, *New Testament Words* (Louisville, KY.: Westminster John Knox Press, 2000), 49

119. "Nobody grows old": Douglas MacArthur, as edited by Suzy Platt, *Respectfully Quoted* (Barnes & Noble, Inc., 1993), 393

120. "If, after my removal": William Carey, as found in http://www.wciujournal.org/monthly/article/william-careys-current-contribution-to-bible-translation-wyclipedia

121. "All labor has value": Martin Luther King, as given by Dr. Rick Rigsby, *Lessons From a Third Grade Dropout* (Nashville, Tenn.: Thomas Nelson, 2006), 59